MACHA'S TWINS

A Spiritual Journey with the Celtic Horse Goddess

Kate Fitzpatrick

Kate Fitzpatrick (signature)

IMMRAM PUBLISHING

Published in June 2017
By Immram Publishing
Inishowen, Donegal, Ireland.
T: +35385 8684190
E: immrampublishing@gmail.com

Cover artwork © Celia Kee Glenane, 2013.
Typesetting and cover design by Joe McAllister of Guildhall Press, Derry.
Author photograph courtesy of Raymond Craig.

© Kate Fitzpatrick 2017

ISBN 978 0 9957983 0 4

Disclaimer
The information in this book is based on the author's personal knowledge and
experience. The techniques for healing and transformation that are described
herein are intended to support the reading of the narrative. This is not a training
manual. If you wish to use any of these techniques, please ensure that you receive
guidance and instruction from a qualified practitioner before doing so.

For my Grandnieces
Abigail, Grace, Emily and Winnie Rose

Contents

Preface

I, Kate Fitzpatrick, am everywoman of today's world who embarks on a quest for the Spiritual Feminine. I am also everywoman and every person who grew up in the North of Ireland in the 1960s, '70s and '80s and lived with the backdrop of 'the Troubles' of that time.

Over the past thirty years, I have studied and taught the spirituality within Celtic myth and delivered workshops, talks and meditations on these themes. My work has been dedicated for many years to building peace in Ireland. In the 1990s and early 2000s I designed workshops with themes from Celtic mythology that were journeys for personal transformation using drama and dance, gestalt process and Jungian psychology. The original workshops were based on the Aran Islands in County Galway and at that time I discovered how to connect with the healing power of landscape. In 1996 I moved to Donegal to bring my work to the North of Ireland.

The journey took me back to the myths of the Ulster Cycle[1] and a call to heal my own Catholic roots within the Northern Irish story. The work evolved over these years and took shape alongside the Peace Process in Northern Ireland. I then realised that there is a link between the land and the need for peace in the North. The emotional memories of all that has happened – the stories of colonisation, famine, and war – are held in the stones, rivers, mountains and lakes and can be divined by those willing to listen and learn.

Macha is the mythical Ulster Goddess who, whilst heavily pregnant, was forced to run a race against the horses of the King of Ulster. She gave birth to twins at the end of the racetrack and cursed the men of Ulster for nine generations, saying they would never have their power when they needed it most. It was Macha who gave her name to the town of Armagh.[2]

The writing of this book comes out of many years of exploring the story of Macha as a healing journey and as a source of transformation in the lives of women. It is the story of my own journey to find the Sacred Feminine and it is also Macha's story of lifting the curse from the men of Ulster. The book is the creation of a new myth around Macha's story in two sections: the search for feminine light and a story of healing in Ulster.

No-one knows what became of Macha. I have used the story that she went back to the Otherworld and took her twins with her. Over the many years of working with Macha, I posed the following questions to women: What was Macha's place in the old stories? As a Mother Goddess and Horse Goddess, where and what is her place today in our lives? How do we call her home to Ulster?

Beginnings

The book started as a series of poems. In March 2012, a month after giving a presentation about Macha at the Navan Centre & Fort in County Armagh[3], I was out at Kinnego beach in Inishowen sitting on a rock enjoying spring sunshine. I heard Macha's voice encouraging me to write her story. She showed me a stream of images and energy patterns that carried the vision of what this book should be about.

In the weeks that followed, Macha's voice continued to speak to me and the style of the book evolved from the images she revealed: *Slow down, you can sense the essence in everything around you. The voice of the stone, the song of the wind. Their nuances speak to you and you begin to make sense of what they are saying. Patterns come to light. A wider mythic story begins to unfold.*

Themes came through each day – the little girl spirits, grandmothers, horses, mothers and daughters, joy, forgiveness and dance. Poems about these themes emerged. The concept of the book spiralled outwards from the poems.

One by one they gradually built into a form and took on an organic flow. It was always circular – repeating and echoing the themes and mythic symbols, crossing over to other worlds in shamanic journeys and translating the images and messages from those journeys into words and story.

I followed the flow of this energy. I collected the poems into groups. Themes became clear. A structure emerged. Chapters took shape. And finally in October 2013 a whole book was completed. At that time, a good friend, skilled in artistic design, went through it with me. Speaking to the creative vision that he saw within the book, he suggested that the poems needed to be opened out to include the images, emotions and nuances of the shamanic journeys that lay behind them. All of these additional stories needed to be brought forth and put into writing.

And so a second process began in March 2014 and has taken three years to complete. I took each section and developed a prose narrative that communicated more of the worlds behind the poems, while still retaining the poetic rhythm of the original script. Following the line through disparate sections and diverse landscapes, and allowing the themes to echo back and forth to each other, I kept going with this process until the full book came together. It expanded greatly in size and finally it was clear that there would be two books contained within one volume: *Healing Feminine Light* and *Healing Light in Ulster*. Both of these titles complement themes from Macha's original story when she cursed the men of Ulster. I realised, too, that this motif of the two books is within the metaphor of the twins in Macha's story. This new story would be her legacy, her gift of forgiveness to Ulster.

Mythic Landscapes Within the Book

Each chapter has a distinct landscape. To enter into these landscapes, you need to surrender into stillness, slow down your breathing and escape the mind's chatter. The voice of essence at the beginning of each chapter will bring you across the threshold and into places of subtle light. Suspend disbelief and cross into the mythic. These are the dreaming landscapes that you will move into. Here you will hear the music of the waves, the cry of the mountain and the whistle of the wind.

Some of the landscapes you travel through are of joy, with music and song. Others are landscapes of pain, rage and grief as women search historical memories in the quest for the divine feminine. Landscapes of nature – mountains, hills, rivers and lakes will speak to you. There are also the dark landscapes of Ulster where the pain and the memories of war are still held. But, within the book, there are also the landscapes of healing, transformation, forgiveness and rebirth.

Healing Feminine Light

The late 1980s and early 1990s were incredible times for women moving into the power of the divine feminine. Western women were plumbing the depths to find, manifest, and express this spirit. This was an era of women who had the courage to make such a journey. To take risks and leave the old forms. To listen to the voices coming up from the depths. To bear witness to remarkable synchronicities. Women at that time made huge leaps forward. Doors opened. Light flowed in. A tidal wave of new beginnings created an uplift of wondrous things. Beautiful forms and unexpected gifts came out of nowhere: a chance meeting, the right book, the song playing on the café speaker. All across Ireland and in the US, I met and worked with women doing this pioneering work.

We stood on the shoulders of the feminists of the '70s who had challenged the gender mores and we took courage from the wild abandon of the women of the '60s who had raised the hems of their skirts and demanded control over their bodies. Those were the women who championed civil rights and forced female issues out into the open in the freedom of a new age. Those women, too, stood on the shoulders of the suffragettes of the early twentieth century, some of whom would become our grandmothers.

Then it was our turn. Drawing upon all who had gone before us, we moved it forward into the realm of spiritual work. We challenged the internalised beliefs that spiritual power belonged only to men and priests. The power of the feminine divine came to find us and meet those who would meet her. We found our own sources of God-in-her and we dared to call the light that was pulsing through us: the Sacred Feminine. We found ways to worship her at sacred sites, holy wells, on mountain tops and beside rivers. In the end it was not worship that she wanted, but partnership.

Delving deep into the shadow of the collective feminine and the collective wounding of several centuries, we dragged images of spiritual women out of the starved depths. They came up from old myths and legends – those stories that formed the archetypal core of western culture. Greek Goddesses, Celtic Goddesses, Great Mothers of Egypt. All appeared on the doorstep or in dreams. Our task was to ground the light that was pouring through us into our bodies and into the earth.[4]

Over the years I met hundreds of women who participated in this quest. Thousands of women were doing this same journey in other lands and cultures. One could see new wisdom in the eyes of strangers. Eyes of women who had made the descent into the dark; suffered the pain; hanged on the nails of shame and power loss. And who, after each journey, returned home to live ordinary lives rearing their children and doing their work in the world.

Our spirit guides in particular were the Celtic Goddesses. They supported all of the work that I was involved in and helped women create personal maps from their own stories and find the way to a healed, new place.

We have many stories to celebrate the feminine light returning to us, to the land and to the soul of cultures. Fragile still is this new light: emerging into changed forms of female spirituality that are now visible in the wider world. The first book of *Macha's Twins* is my story of this journey.

Healing Light in Ulster

The second book of *Macha's Twins* is about the land and heart of Ulster. It is the continued journey with Macha who wishes to bring healing light to the North of Ireland, a place that even in mythical time was associated with war.[5]

As I continued to write, the backdrop of this new mythic story of Ulster was changing every month, moving forward with me all through the years between 2011 and 2015.

No longer working just with women on a spiritual quest, I was meeting with people from diverse groups – business circles, coaching events, music sessions and horse-riding lessons. Across the North of Ireland, a broad arc of people and places was drawn into this second journey as the mythic dimensions behind ordinary events began to show themselves. The energy for this story was very different.

The years of intense transformation work with women gave way to an influx of a subtle, translucent light; discernible behind the scenes of the gatherings I was witness to. The ordinary landscapes of Ulster became fertile ground for Macha's healed light to take root. Everyday events became sacred, resonating at the edges with this golden glow, as diverse groups became part of the mythological story.

I crossed into the nature kingdoms where rivers and mountains sang to me. They told me of their sorrow in the holding of memories from the past. I went back in time to witness events of the past and I crossed into altered states to have conversations with ancestors, long dead, who came to meet me with stories that needed to be told.

I saw the light moving through the culture around me. I witnessed the power of music to clear the land. I saw the sweetness of song soften the hearts of the men of Ulster. I used crystals to assist in the healing of the land and joined with other crystal and shamanic energy workers to create mandalas for healing the collective soul. The power of horses and spirit horses moved through each chapter with me as I witnessed more and more of the feminine light returning to the land of Ulster.

The concept of holding the tension of opposites is a core principle within Jungian psychology. If you can hold the tension in a creative way, for long enough and without sinking into either side of the conflict, a new solution, a transcendent, will emerge from deep within the psyche. It will be a healing symbol and it will have the numinous power to unite the opposites and let energy flow again at a higher level of vibration. The pathway for this to happen is called the 'transcendent function'.[6]

You can apply this principle to the soul of groups, cultures and nations as much as to the psyche of an individual. In the second book of *Macha's Twins*, it is the power of music, crystal healing and horse wisdom that join together to become a trio of transcendent forces, opening the way for rebirth.

As I write these words, the Northern Ireland Assembly has just had an election for a new government and, on the surface, it looks as though we might be going back down the slippery slope into the impasse of 'Orange' and 'Green'.[7]

Time will tell if it will be the women of the North who will join with Macha and her twins to create a transcendent pathway out of this conflict of opposites and into a new mythology for Ulster.

Kate Fitzpatrick, March 2017

BOOK ONE

Healing Feminine Light

PART I
Macha's Curse

CHAPTER ONE
Calling Macha Home

Irish Mythology is far from dead.
It springs to life from the essence of the land,
From the changing moods of the weather,
From the magic created by a sudden ray of sunlight
Or a small, barely visible, rainbow over a still lake.
Myth springs to life in the colours and smiles
And heartfelt warmth of the people on this land,
A softness and gentleness that creates its own magic.
Myth springs to life in modern poetry
That still holds an understanding of a timeless past.
In the rich nuances of life
Carried in the names of places and songs,
Myth tells the story of our evolving soul.

February 2012, Armagh

There are times when you know you have come round full circle and there is a sense of completion. You can reach out and put your finger on the spot where you started. Taking a pulse to define an important moment. The story of Macha is like that. A cyclical tale, from an ancient myth, brought forward in time. Macha speaks across the mists of history, resonating with the lives of women today, to guide and assist, heal and transform that which is beyond words in the everyday language we use.

There is an ancient myth of Macha that tells of her place in the history of Ireland. She is the Horse Goddess who cursed the men of Ulster. And, as myths stay alive in the soul of a people across the veils of the Otherworld, there is also the living Macha, present with us always. *Calling Macha Home* is a redeemed place in the feminine soul, carrying forgiveness and release from an ancient curse.

Navan Fort outside Armagh is situated in the place known as Emain Macha, meaning the 'Twins of Macha'.[1] This is the place in Ulster, within the symbolic landscape of myth, where past and present can meet to give us a renewed and contemporary sense of the spirit of Macha.

A chance meeting with the staff of the Navan Centre & Fort in July 2011 revealed our shared interest in Macha. The Centre had reopened after several years of closure and was being run by a dynamic team, all of who were interested in the Macha of Emain Macha. As a result of our conversation, I was invited to make a presentation in February 2012 with the title: *Calling Macha Home*.

In the weeks before I made the presentation, I could see the spirit of Macha galloping on a horse across the plains of Ireland towards Emain Macha. I sensed the momentous power of her returning to the ancient sacred site in County Armagh that was named after her. Her desire joined with mine to make this truly a homecoming. In those weeks before the talk, she assured me: *I will meet you there.*

I gathered all of what might be of interest to a general audience. It would be a testing through the public eye. I asked myself: *Will it hold?* I wanted to know whether the journeys of women's healing over many years, alongside Macha's original story, would be received. I wanted to give the whole story back to the wider community of the Northern province. I knew it would be deepened and strengthened by this retelling in the very heart of the Armagh landscape.

On the day of the talk I arrive by lunchtime and walk from the car park towards the Navan Centre. Partially hidden by trees and shrubs, it is a circular stone building with a turf roof. As I grasp the brass handle and open the heavy oak door, I have the sense of crossing a threshold into another world. Beyond the entrance hall is a bright circular atrium that serves as a focal point in the interpretative centre. A circle of thick wooden pillars surrounds the open floor space. My eye is drawn upwards where daylight floods in above me. I pause and look at the series of paintings positioned just below the circular windows in the roof. Depicting the story of the Ulster battles of old, they show Cú Chulainn, King Conchobhar and Medhbh, in the rough-hewn colours of red and brown with an occasional shaft of yellow that animates a face.[2]

I am welcomed by one of the staff. There are many interpretative centres in Ireland that cater for the tourist; ordinary and organised, with everything boxed into its place in history. Maps and fixed smiles to welcome you. But it was different here. Rather, in this place, the people who greet you come forth with the shining magic of ancient times in their very aura.

I am guided to a table in the restaurant area and joined by three of the staff. The smell of coffee hangs in the air and I am offered food in a most gracious manner. The ensuing conversation has the dynamic tempo of a team of players known to each other, but long since apart, converging again with a common aim that sparks the core passions of all.

After this welcome and lunch, I take leave of my hosts as they return to work and I go outside, walk over the path, and start to climb the green hill of Emain Macha. A gentle wind blows around me as I connect with the spirits of the land. I know the history. This is the ancient mound that housed the Kings of Ulster in Cú Chulainn's time. And before that it was dedicated to the Goddess of fertility and birth. Her presence is still held in the green roundness of the hill.

I notice the circle of trees around the base of the hill. Hazel, ash and oak amongst others. Bleak and bare they are, at this time in early February, but a breath of spring is also to be felt here today and I give thanks for it. I ask permission from the trees to enter the space and align my purpose with the spirits of the land. Thus given, I join with them to create a circle of protection around the work. I see nothing yet of Macha here. But her presence is strong and I sense her waiting. *I am here*, I whisper to her and to the winds that hold all.

In the late afternoon, I return to the building to help with the layout of the space. We set out fifty chairs in three semi-circles around the wooden pillars of the atrium and leave the centre empty to act as an area for performance. We test the lighting and I move around, speaking and singing to determine the best position from which to deliver the talk. It is the women of the Centre who afterwards will say, that at the moment when I placed the table for my things on the side of the space, the whole atmosphere changed. They will tell me that the building stopped being one thing and started to become something else. I look again at the wooden pillars in the half-light of evening and see that they are alive and breathing with the same quiet pulse that I felt on the land.

I leave to go and rest for a short while. I return, dressed now for the role of performance, and sit quietly waiting for it all to begin. The Centre manager and another young man are present with me in the waiting time. Watching them both calls to mind the dignity of the Gaelic princes of old and I smile to think how much the myths live so handsomely in all of the staff here.

As folk begin to arrive, I chat for a while with them, finding out how far they have travelled and listening to what they might expect from the evening. Standing back, I watch as the staff greet people and show them around. The large space is warm and welcoming. Lighting has been adjusted to create an atmosphere that shimmers with the feel of something ancient and Celtic.

I look over at the women of the Centre and see them as queens of Navan Fort. One with long dark hair and a strong presence is not unlike Macha herself as she leads the guests to the tea in the restaurant area. Another woman with short hair, her brown eyes twinkling with both intelligence and mischief, is chatting amiably and taking photographs as she goes around. I watch the men of the staff team standing and greeting people in various corners of the space. They glow with the quiet dignity of ancient royal hosts. In their confidence, humour and generous welcome to the folk arriving, they are like princes of the Tuatha Dé Danann. In this practised hospitality the place becomes an ancient stronghold of Celtic Ulster with guests arriving for an evening celebration. When people are conducted to their seats, there is a hush that settles itself over the whole place.

Standing behind the circles of chairs where the audience is now seated, I listen to the introduction by the MC for the evening. He is a man with sparkling blue eyes and his energy resonates back through the mists of time to where he might have been a wise druid, a talented bard. With great dignity, he carefully gathers the energy of the people and creates an air of anticipation: 'It is indeed an historical event to have this talk about Macha at the Centre tonight. We, the staff here, have been working with these stories of the Ulster myths for many years. As you may know, the story of Macha is central to the whole way the Ulster myths played out in those ancient times.'

I gather myself and walk into the performance space. I stand in stillness waiting for the moment to speak. There is a sense of emptiness and uncertainty. I stand back and allow this to be, wondering: *Where do I need to start?*

There were three Machas in Irish mythology.[3] The one of most interest here tonight is the Macha who was the Horse Goddess of the Tuatha Dé Danann. She gave her name to this place now called Navan Fort. She said it would carry the name of her children forever. And so it has been known for time immemorial as Emain Macha, the Twins of Macha.[4]

Taking up my fiddle, I step into the centre space and play. The emptiness dissipates, a flow comes in and we are carried into the magic of the evening. I begin to tell the original story of Macha:

Macha arrived out of nowhere, it seemed, and walked into Cruinniuc's house in a stately and proud manner. He was a prosperous farmer who lived in a remote fort in the hills of Ulster. His wife had died and left him with four children and he lived on his farm with his children and his servants. Macha did not speak to Cruinniuc when she entered his house. She sat down on a stool and said nothing for many hours, simply staring into the fire.

A woman of great dignity and proud bearing, she was beautifully dressed and had an air of elsewhere about her. She was from the Otherworld, one of the divine race of the Tuatha Dé Danann. When mealtime came, she got up and went to the kitchen to prepare food. Later, as night fell, she piled up the ashes on the fire. She went to Cruinniuc's room and lay down with him. In this way she became his wife.

Macha stayed with Cruinniuc for many years and he, for the first time since his wife died, was content. Macha loved him and his children thrived under her care. His farm prospered and there was a gaiety about the place. She brought in the light of the Tuatha Dé Danann from the realm beyond the waves.[5]

I stop and allow the words to resonate. Walking slowly around the central space, I am pacing myself and sensing the impact of this story on the people in the audience.

After the pause, I step closer to the front again and continue:

There came a day of an assembly and celebrations at the King of Ulster's domain – a hill and a fort on this very land where we stand tonight, in the south of County Armagh. It was at Samhain time, which marked the end of the Celtic year and celebrated the harvest. In those days, there were many such gatherings at auspicious times of the year, where women and men would go to be entertained with games and sport, feasting and music. Often they stayed for several days at a time.

Macha begged Cruinniuc not to go. She thought it would bring trouble to them. Sheepishly, he said he was going anyway. This brought on a silence to Macha. She warned him as he was preparing to leave: 'Whatever you do there, do not speak of our shared life here. On no account are you to speak of me. Do not mention my name to anyone, or our time together will be over.'

Cruinniuc replied: 'Of course not. What we have created is too precious to lose. You can rest assured, I will say not a word.' He smiled at her tenderly. 'Very well, do as you will,' said Macha and she turned and left him.

Many games and celebrations, much music and cheer, took place on that day. The highlight was the racing of the horses, running in pairs and driven by a charioteer. Won, as always, by the King's own finest mares. People were praising them: 'There is no finer pair in the whole country, and none could run swifter than these!'

But sadly Cruinniuc, carried away with the excitement of the day, boasted about Macha. He said that his wife could run faster than the King's horses. There was shock indeed at this declaration. The King was beside himself with rage: 'Summon that woman to me now. We'll see what she is able to do against my two finest mares.'

Messengers were sent to Macha's homestead. Showing her pregnant belly, she begged them to come back when she had given birth to her child. She was greatly dismayed that Cruinniuc had done such a thing. 'I am sorry, Madam, if you don't run the race, your husband will be killed,' the messengers said to her. 'Ah, foolish Cruinniuc,' she said. She sighed and shook her head, throwing on her cloak to go.

Macha arrived at the royal racetrack. She pleaded with the King and begged him to show mercy and let her give birth to her child. 'I am near my time,' she said, 'I will run the race with your horses after I deliver my child.' But the King refused: 'You will do as I say, woman. You will run the race now or your husband will be killed.'

Macha felt the shock ripple through her whole body, realising that on a matter of pride he was actually going to force her to do this. Alas, in the realm of the King's sovereignty, there was too much at stake to let her away with this. His power and the fertility of the land were based on the superior performance of his horses. He would punish her husband for his foolish boast.

Macha took a deep breath and turned around to face the crowd of Ulster men and women. She took slow paces towards them and spoke with a desperate quiver in her voice, pleading with them: 'A mother bore each of you, help me now, please ... help me.' But no-one stood out to help her, woman nor man. Pointing at her swollen belly, they jeered and mocked her, adding to the rising tide of ridicule that was now gathering power over their sense of judgement.[6]

I pause again and look at the people gathered in front of me. All are listening intently. Together, we are knowing and feeling the truth of this story. Macha's spirit is now tangibly in the room. Her pain, her pleas, the reality of who she was and what she did. I sense her presence standing at the wooden pillars to the right of me. Pregnant, strong and vital, shaking with emotion. Her eyes flash with anger and fear, watering at the sides of them. Her swollen face is flushed; tendrils of hair are stuck to the sweat on her cheeks. Her head is moving rapidly and she has the look of a hunted animal.

I take a few minutes of silence, acknowledging her presence in our midst. Taking a deep breath, I continue with the story at the ancient royal racetrack:

Macha said to all present: 'You will pay dearly for this, you men of Ulster, for showing no respect for a woman in my condition.' Turning to Cruinniuc, she said: 'I will run this race to save your life but I will not return to your home.' She turned and faced the King again: 'You will not win this one, King of Ulster, I can assure you of that. I am Macha, a daughter of Sainrith mac Imbaith, and a divine Queen of the Tuatha Dé Danann. You will pay for the cruelty you have shown me today. From now on, this place will bear my name and that of my children, and all men who watch here will be punished for this humiliation of a woman with child.'[7]

Macha raised herself to a larger stature and walked to the starting line. Defiant and bright, she was smiling now. When the gong sounded, she took off like a lightning bolt. Running at the speed of the wind, her hair spread out in a great fan behind her. Her belly was as light as though held by wings. You could see her legs move in fourfold as she sped down the track, well ahead of the King's horses. She won the race and collapsed in a heap at the finishing line. Screaming out with the pangs of labour, she gave birth to twin babies: a boy and a girl.

After they came out of her she issued forth a roar, terrifying to hear. It reverberated for miles across the land. In her outrage, she drew down a curse of great magnitude on all of the men of Ulster. Those present fell immediately to the ground, writhing in pain. She issued this fate to them: 'Men of Ulster, you will never have your power when you need it most. You will be as vulnerable as a woman in labour. For five days and four nights you will suffer these pains. When you go into battle, you will become the laughing stock of the warriors of Ireland. You will suffer this humiliation over and over for nine generations for what you have done to me today.'

And with that, Macha left them and took her babies with her. She was never again seen in south Ulster.

Both of her prophecies came true. The place became known as Emain Macha, the Twins of Macha, and all through the Ulstermen's battles with Medhbh, the mighty Queen of Connaught, their power deserted them and they were struck down with the pangs of Macha when they needed to fight.[8]

When the whole story has been told, I take up my fiddle and play. The music fills the air with feeling, touches the heart, and allows the truth of the words to settle with all present. When the last strands of reverberation have died away, I put my instrument down and step out of the centre space, making room for Macha's spirit to settle and find her place in the midst of this gathering of people.

As her presence enters the space again, I see relief in her eyes and a faint softness about her mouth. She is looking out at the audience with gratitude. I realise as I look at her belly that she is not pregnant now, but strong and fit, dressed in a robe of royal ruby and gold. Her long hair is shining thick and black, and her mouth is poised in a gentle smile. Around her head is a tinge of golden light. It is the kind of light that comes to those who have suffered much but come through the harrowing to a vulnerable sense of peace.

I look at the group gathered in front of me. I see acceptance and warmth in their eyes, and I realise that the whole epic of Macha's story has been received here: the old, the new, and the future possibilities for healing. Yes indeed, the story does hold up in the public eye; the testing is complete. The spirit of a Goddess has entered this room.

CHAPTER TWO
Conversations at Emain Macha

Poetry flows
From a source
Beyond logic.
In a dance from myth
To possible reality
And back again,
We create a pathway
That lets us ask
The question:
How is this story of Macha
Still relevant
In our society today?

February 2012, Armagh

After a break for tea, we gather again in the circular space held within the wooden pillars. I pull a chair into the middle of the floor and ask for questions or comments about the story. The excitement is palpable and from everyone present there is a commitment to stay.

I sit and look at all present. There are people from many places in the North. Landscapes of different lives come into the room. An ocean of questions, a respect from all. I notice the softness in the faces of the men. The shine in the eyes of the women. The attention to listen. The wisdom that is coming forth. A collective spirit digging down into the heart of this story.

With profound respect from both the women and men, we speak across the room to each other, asking questions for clarity and entering into an animated discussion. The conversation continues, moving rapidly from subject to subject. Like the waves on a beach, the questions come in, spill onto the shore. And all search through the debris to find the treasures that have been washed up before each wave retreats to the sea.

Nine is a magical number. It is three times three. Count the waves. Beyond the ninth wave is an entrance to the Otherworld. Manannán mac Lir guards this threshold to the mystical realms of the Sídhe and the Goddesses. These are the places where the divine race of the Tuatha Dé Danann resides. Count the waves.

One

Women in the audience speak candidly of the spiritual search to find themselves. They add poignant depth and truth to the conversation: immediacy in their identity with Macha. There is a quiet presence from the women staff of Navan Fort. They sit, with confidence and delight, listening to these stories brought to life. In their ease, they hold the space for all. A silent power, the female force of Navan Fort. Strength, stillness, serenity.

Two

Here tonight are three men from the heart of Ulster. That central plain of land spreading west from Lough Neagh to the Sperrin Mountains. These men are skilled in the healing arts and have great respect for nature's wisdom. They know the magic in the soul of the land. They share their insights with sparkling humour.

Three

One woman, who seems sceptical about the whole story, asks in evident frustration: 'But why is she the Horse Goddess?' In response to this I speak of how Macha won the race with a power and vitality equal to the horses. I compare her to Epona, the Horse Goddess of Europe, and to Rhiannon, her Welsh counterpart.[1] Horses were sacred to the Celts and were always under the protection of a specific Goddess.

But it is a hard question to address and I throw it open to the audience. I see others looking at each other, eager to answer. Three of the male staff at Navan Fort are animated and excited. They lean in with answers from their fine knowledge of the Ulster myths. I see all of the people around me enjoying this dance of words as new ideas emerge, like sparks of fire, throughout the room.

But it is best to answer truly this profound question from the instinct within. Leave behind the words that are written down by scribes over the centuries. Macha was, and still is, the Horse Goddess because her female spirit was akin to that of an unbroken horse. Wild, free and strong. She could run fast and never became prey to the dominant male power of the day.

I look over to my right and I see Macha sitting beside

the people closest to the door in the west. Her eyes are glistening with tears at the warm welcome she is receiving here from a crowd of Ulster folk. I have seen her many times in other gatherings of women in remote retreat centres by the sea or in the hills. But never like this; in a public place within the six counties of Northern Ireland. She is indeed a Goddess presence in our midst tonight.

Four

A man practised in quiet wisdom speaks on the nature of myth: 'It is an oral sculpture and therefore cannot be defined by reason or logic. Myth is fluid and changes its shape over time.'

As he says this, everything in the room starts to vibrate. I sense the undercurrent of our night making its presence felt. Numinous. We are all healing as we speak. Women and men together sharing here. We are in the old myth completely, believing its truth and, at the same time, pushing through to a new one.

Five

A young man trying to get his head around the whole story, sincerely asks: 'But why did she come back when she was treated so badly?' People turn round to look at him. A pause. Another powerful question for all to address. There are many possible places to go with this; several people are leaning in to offer a contribution. The women in particular are trying to explain that paradox that we all know: no matter what happens, the desire to come home and to look for the best in any situation is always within us. We hold a willingness to forgive as part of our nature.

The question, however, shifts us all to a bigger picture. *Why would Macha want to come back to Ulster?* People flow in with various possibilities, responding easily from within the story itself. *Perhaps to lift the curse? How will she claim her place again? What about forgiveness – can that ever come here to this province? What a difficult circumstance for a woman to give birth in. What happened to the twins?*

Six
This leads us into a whole consideration of women and birthing. A bright-faced man who has a lot to say offers another angle on this. He recalls his mother talking about the tradition of 'churching'. Up until the Second Vatican Council in 1962, Catholic women were obliged to go into the church for a ritual of purification after they had given birth to a baby.[2] Some folks are shaking their heads that such a tradition could ever have existed, never mind up to such a recent date.

Seven
On a more humorous note, local stories and folklore are told. The Armagh Gaelic football team believe that it is the curse of Macha that has caused their failure over the years to bring home the All-Ireland senior title, with only one win in 2002 to their name since 1887. You could picture these big strong men in the Armagh colours of orange and white, sitting around in the changing room after a match, shaking their heads in disappointment and wondering: 'Will she will ever leave us alone and let us get on with winning the cup?'

Eight
A man sitting in the front row asks about the large Rose Quartz crystal that is sitting on the floor in front of me. I know from chatting earlier that he and his wife have travelled all the way from Donaghadee to Armagh this evening. They heard about the talk on Radio Ulster last Saturday morning and were interested to come and find out more. As I listen to him speak so profoundly about the healing power of crystals, I look at the pink stone on its stand of oak,

glistening brightly. It was given to me to support my work in Donegal and the North at a ceremony for *Light in Ireland* in 2007, dedicated for healing and harmony.[3]

Nine

We talk of Lough Neagh, the lake in the centre of the province, and of the druids and saints who lived close by its waters. We imagine the pilgrims who would have travelled the roads from Emain Macha to the lough. As many of the northern counties touch its shore, it holds a central place in the geography of the land. As an entry to the Otherworld, Lough Neagh was believed to have magical properties, lending itself to the stories of the mythical beings that lived there. It is as though all of us are pilgrims walking along forgotten old tracks. We are going up many roads together, and crossing over stiles and bridges. We are walking through forests of old and fields of new.

As our voices move in and out of the centre space, a pattern of energy is weaving through the room in a pulsing flow of new life. Like water, at once cleansing and renewing, it is flowing in from every corner of the North from where the people here have travelled. A hologram of energy. A mandala of light and love. A mythical pattern created by the rhythm of questions, answers and debate. The pauses, the voices, the spaces. The presence of Macha in the room with us. The dignity, the beauty of people here. The emotion, the intelligence. The shared history. Witnessing something profound. Alchemy of myth reborn.

On the following morning, a group of four women from Monaghan, and a companion of mine, join me to do a meditation at the Emain Macha Centre. Gathered on chairs and wrapped in warm blankets, we call the spirit of Macha into the room. And, as each person asks this Mother Goddess for a healing intention, Macha comes in with a gentle light.

Afterwards, my companion waits behind in the room to hold and witness the space whilst we five women go outside. We walk along the back lane in silence, cross the road and begin to climb the hill. Around the base of the ancient mound, the old trees are welcoming us.

Without words, we each spread out and find our way to the top. We are gathering the magic that was woven last night by all present. Through our bodies, and with song and music, we dance the spirit of Macha back into the land, in the presence of spring sunshine and a peach-coloured aura of women's light.

I sense the presence of an ancient guardian spirit held in the stones, the circle of the trees and in the wind. She appears in the form of a druidic priestess, wearing a robe of silver and pale blue. Her long grey hair glistens in the spring light. She stares at me through eyes of startling blue and nods slowly in approval. Her voice speaks out clearly to us:

Awaken again the power of this land
And Macha's place in it.
Heal the mythic memory held here and
Undo the pattern of cursing men.
Lift the out-worn symbols with the joy of dance
And the land will remember your name.

CHAPTER THREE
A Deeper Story

Slow down,
You can sense the essence
In everything around you.
The voice of the stone,
The song of the wind.
Their nuances speak to you
And you begin to make sense
Of what they are saying.
Patterns are revealed
And made clear.
It is from this place
That a mythic story begins to unfold.
Everything around vibrates with it
And is woven into the substance
That gives it life.

March 2012, Donegal

At the end of March, almost seven weeks since the talk at Emain Macha, I decide to write a book on Macha.

The place where I write is a little house along a laneway out in the country, a few miles from Moville. There is an old farmyard below the lane and the land around me is called Tirrion. In the stones and the running waters within the valley below me here, Tirrion holds the magic of stillness. It is a place of deep peace and carries the soft light of other realms and fairy folk. This is a rich green glen in Inishowen, in the county of Donegal. It is rooted in the land of Ulster. The original nine-county Ulster of the mythic era.[1]

Each morning I go to the beach to walk. I sit on a rock to take in the quiet calm and give thanks for all. No matter what the day – sun or rain, warm or cold – I am at peace here. I breathe in the sea air and begin my T'ai Chi flow of movements. Each posture takes me to a deeper place of stillness within. The secret of T'ai Chi is to move as slowly as you possibly can. Slowly, slowly, moving your hands. No thoughts. The waves come and go. You breathe. The images are alive in your hands: *Parting the Clouds – Pushing the Waves – Flying Wild Goose*. In this pulse of life, you become one with all of nature around you.[2]

Waves are coming in. They are ever moving towards the shore. Driven by the power of the ocean currents and the wind. I sense the presence of Macha in the thunderous power of the white horses. She is riding on the top of the waves.

I am at one with the spirit of Macha. Her voice blends with my thoughts and resonates with the voice within me. It is a voice that rises from the body. Within this silence and harmony with nature, I begin to hear a deeper truth. Reflecting on all of her story, there are still questions that might be asked: *What was the depth of rage that caused her to put such a curse on the men of Ulster? Did anyone help her when she was giving birth at the finishing line? What became of her twin babies?*

In the stillness I watch a seagull swoop, making its slow flight across the bay. I walk back along the shore noticing the scattered fronds of seaweed and the old footprints from yesterday's day-trippers. I return to my car and drive up the road to the house. After a cup of tea, I begin to formulate in words the essence of what was communicated to me on the beach.

Macha sits beside me and tells her story. As I listen to her words, I am shown scenes of what happened that day she ran the race. It is like watching a film on a screen in front of me:

'Before the full dawning of the new era of Kings and warriors, some men put great value on the sweetness that was possible in shared love with a woman who chose them over any other. In my love for Cruinniuc, I brought this quality back to Ulster. The King sensed from Cruinniuc's boast that I, his wife, was no ordinary woman. It was a threat to his sovereignty if his horses were not the swiftest of the land.'

Listening to Macha, I can see again the scene before the race and I hear what the King is saying to her. I see him stomping around in his anger. He is looking at her stricken face as she turns back from the crowd:

'We'll see what that woman is able to do against my two finest mares. We will be greatly entertained by this spectacle. And no upstart farmer will dare again to make a laughing stock out of me.'

Macha continues:

'He hardly noticed that I was pregnant. He was sneering at me, and with his words, betraying the emptiness of himself: "I care nothing for who you say you are. You will run this race and run it *now*." He saw only the wild spirit of defiance and all he wanted was submission from a brazen woman who was daring to defy his command. He thought it would be impossible for me to win. He was already savouring the satisfaction of having me crushed. But my fury was building and I made a decision: *I will leave a mark on this place and on these people that will last forever.* And, for the sake of every woman alive, I had to find the physical strength to actually win the race and outwit him in his bid for power over the sacred rights of women.

'I called on the Tuatha Dé Danann, my people across the waves. Goddesses and divine sisters, queens of mighty warrior status, princes of the Otherworld, brothers in spirit. They all came in on horses, proudly carrying themselves. Their golden light streaming out behind them. The horses of Manannán mac Lir appeared out of the air and reared up with a terrifying screech. I pulled their power into my belly and with all of this support, I ran like the horses of the wild.'

Sitting listening to Macha and watching this scene unfold, I see that the crowd watched all this and were gasping in horror. I see Macha walking to the starting line defiant and bright. She is smiling. I glance over at Macha sitting in my room today. She turns and looks directly into my eyes. Her eyes penetrate right into the core of me as she talks:

'Can you imagine the force a woman can summon up if threatened at the moment before giving birth? Can you imagine the power of the heavens and earth supporting her to protect her young? That will tell you the full force of the curse that I issued.

'My rage against the King was the fury of a woman deeply betrayed by the misuse of power. To herself, her womb, to her babies and to her mate. A woman feels rage like this when she has been violated to her core.'

Macha turns away and continues with her story:

'The mares of the King were twin foals. Unusual enough. Such foals are believed to be gifts from the divine world and bring a great blessing for the fertility of the land. They were almost identical in colour; dark brown with traces of black in their coats. One had a white band on her face. They grew into magnificent animals. Beautiful and sleek. Highly prized for their magical powers, as well as their racing skill. People mostly respected that power. But times were changing and some were starting to treat horses as mere beasts to be yoked and trained, losing respect for their superb intelligence and innate dignity.

'The twin mares were supporting me that day. Even though we raced against each other, we were together in a run for freedom. That, too, might be remembered someday. Afterwards, when my young had spilled out onto the mud, the horses watched me on the ground. Neighed and signalled. Moving their heads up and down, they whinnied over to me, bringing in strength. Although no-one in the crowd helped, I was not alone.'

I ask her: 'What became of you and your twin babies?' After a pause, the story of Macha's leaving unfolds in front of me.

The air is hushed and a deep sadness prevails as Macha lies on the ground after the babies have been born. She waves her hands over the heads of the babies, joining them forever to this place that will bear their names. She doesn't move for a long time, allowing the afterbirth to be disgorged from her body. She scrapes in the earth with a sharp stone to make a hole to bury this part of her, so her blood mingles with the soil. No woman has come to her aid, cowered now by the events of the day and afraid they also would fall victim to the King's need to punish someone for this terrible scream that Macha has uttered. She uses the stone to cut the cords and utters a blessing for the earth.

As she gathers up her babies to her breast, the crowd in silence watch and time stands still. She says nothing to anyone. You can hear a deep lament coming from the trees on the other side of the lake. It is the ones from the Otherworld, the Dananns, who are in mourning for what has been lost to the people.

Macha pulls herself to her feet, still holding the babies in her arms. She walks a few paces to where Cruinniuc is standing. She holds his gaze for quite some time and with tears in her eyes she nods at him, affirming all that had been good between them. In this exchange, her eyes say that the sadness of this parting is not his fault. He was a man broken down by a King. Who could blame him for such a mistake? No, not Macha, she had loved him, although it was the end for them. He would be without her now.

Macha is leaving and everything she stood for in the sacredness and dignity of women is being lost to the whole of Ulster. The women in the crowd hang their heads in shame. She looks over to where the King is on the ground at the side of the track writhing in great pain. He is stunned into silence by these strange events. The horror that a woman actually gave birth on his noble racetrack is too much for him to bear. In all its awfulness, it would be him now that people will mock and scorn. He has the grace to look stricken, realising too late what he has done – not just in destroying Cruinniuc, but in this terrible affliction he has brought down on the warriors of Ulster. The curse will indeed keep them weak in many battles from this day on.

The King senses, too, that he has deeply offended the old ways of the people. He knows not what, but the resonance of her words is still vibrating within him. It scares him – the power of her scream lingering on.

Macha turns to him with scorn and smiles coldly. It has been a sad but necessary victory for her. She looks now at the crowd and shakes her head slowly at them, displaying an obvious disbelief that good people could be so stupid. The grief that has come over the whole place is shocking to behold. Everyone senses that something precious is being lost. All who watched the race know that they have participated in the humiliation of a woman at her most sacred time, that of bringing in the new-born.

Macha looks over once more at the ground where her birth's blood has seeped into the earth, marking forever the place where a pregnant woman was forced to run a race against the horses of the King of Ulster. You can hear a haunting song from her as she moves across the land: *The land will remember my blood; the place will bear the name of my children.*

The song of the Otherworld gets louder. The crowd shiver with the haunting melody that is calling Macha away from this place. She turns her back on all of them and slowly, carrying her twins, she walks towards the trees beside the lake. A swirling mist is moving across the land. Walking into the distance, her figure gets smaller and smaller.

The King knows she has beaten him. He looks over at Cruinniuc with a pang of regret for what he has destroyed. But too late. Cruinniuc has already turned his back on the King and is looking towards the place where Macha is going. He weeps tears into the soft mist that now envelops them all.

The eerie silence lasts a long time. A feeling of despair

spreads through the crowd and fear is struck in their hearts. The spell is broken only when some people stoop to gather their things and shuffle off towards the gates to go home. The warriors are writhing on the ground; it seems in slow motion now. It will be a long time indeed before the men of Ulster will be free of Macha's curse.

As Macha approaches the trees, you can hear the loud rustle of the wind moving through them. Their branches become like fingers and hands reaching out for her. They become large arms that fold Macha and the babies into them. She vanishes from sight completely.

As the daylight fades, a Samhain twilight brings in an emptiness to everything, making those few remaining folk shudder. Finally, there is only the sound of flapping wings and two swans fly out, circle around the lake, and then disappear back into the mist.

I sit in silence when these pictures fade. I am aware again of Macha beside me. I have no words. She reaches over and grasps my hand and says: 'Now you understand the deeper story. The babies went back to the Otherworld on the back of those swans and a white horse came for me. We have lived out beyond the ocean's nine waves for generations of time.'

October 2012, Donegal

Over the months in dialogue with Macha, deeper levels of her story emerge. More questions have been answered. I spent early mornings at the beach watching the waves, then returned to the little house to sit at the table and find the words to describe the pictures she had shown me. As the seasons turned, a healing was achieved. The damaging power of the King has been released from her story. Purged, transformed, forgiven.

I smudge the room with sage,
To clear it
Of the heaviness
That surfaces
When the King's role
In Macha's story
Is under consideration.
As I look at the bowl of bright pink roses
On the windowsill,
I can see a moment in time
When innocence will be returned
To women and young girls,
Once the old burden
Of male shame
Is flushed out of
Female bodies and souls.
I stand motionless for a few moments
And, as light comes into the room,
I hear, in the otherworldly stillness,
A little girl singing
In the field beyond my window.
It gladdens my heart,
And I smile
At the beauty of flowers in a bowl,
Brightened by afternoon sunshine.

PART II
Initiation

CHAPTER FOUR
Fertile Blood

The ancients believed
That a woman's womb blood is sacred.
The onset of menstruation brought forth the maiden.
The birth blood marked a passage to motherhood,
And the ceasing of blood at menopause
Was the initiation into the wisdom of the crone.

The call for any woman
To go and search for feminine light
Would be a descent into the darkness.
It will be a death of all beliefs within you
That stand in the way of finding the truth.
If you can hold all of this,
And re-emerge in your new self.
The ancient wisdom you sought,
Will flow in every cell of your body.

Spring 1990, Sligo

The blood flows though me. I am hunkered down, releasing it onto the earth. I watch and see it sit, glistening red on the peat soil. The blood ready to nourish new life is gone now. The loss is deep. What does it mean to me and my love in the yearning we have to create life beyond us?

As I watch the blood flow onto the dark peat soil and scrubby heather under me, I am deepening into another place. Going within my womb, I try and understand the truth beneath the grief. On the top of Knocknarea Mountain I begin to sense the power of female blood for renewal, transformation and rebirth. Glimpsing the hidden mysteries, I join myself with the power of ancient female bones buried here beneath me.

Our house has a panoramic view of Sligo Bay. At low tide, the plain of sand stretches a few miles out in front. On spring mornings you can see the sun rise over in the east behind the mountains in the distance. Keelogyboy and Crockauns.

We have horses at our house. My favourite is Joanne, a big cream-coloured mare. Joanne, my niece's horse, is stabled with us for several months. My husband is superbly gifted in the handling of horses. Sensitive and alert, he moves in and out of their world, in an easy-going and practical way. I have watched him gallop across a beach where the power of him and the horse together was a beauty so profound, that it brought tears to my eyes. I have learned a lot about horses from him over the years. This has instilled in me a confidence to just get up and go.

I am on Joanne riding across the strand. The tide is out. I have crossed the channel at Walter's Lane and am now heading for the stone pillars that mark out the road over to Coney Island. It is passable at low water. I have cramps in my womb. I am in pain and my heart is sore. Another flow of menstrual blood means there will be no baby this month. It has taken me down, yet again, into the emptiness. Joanne's pace is picking up. I am holding on tight. She is in control, not I, but I trust her completely. Fit and able and in no way afraid, I have surrendered to the moment. The wind takes my hair and the pounding of hooves across the sand becomes my chant for freedom.

As we approach the low-water line, at the far end of a long stretch of beach, I rein her in to slow down. I am breathless and exhilarated. Something deep has shifted. The grief is not so sore, and the stitching cramps are gone. I reach over to stroke the side of my horse, laughing and talking to her. *Thank you so much for all of this.* We turn around and walk for a while, moving slowly through the softer sand. Catching our breath and letting the power settle, we make our way gently back across the strand and wade through the 'gut' before the tide turns.

When we return to the house I am at peace. What a gift has been given. To trust my own body and the horse's wisdom, and be able somehow in this surrender to transform the pain into ecstasy and pure joy. The healing offered by this horse is a new experience. I glimpse an unfolding story. In these few months of spring moving into summer, I ride often with Joanne. Sometimes out trotting like a dance. On calmer days just walking along the sand. Another time with a friend on a horse beside us, we go to visit people on Coney Island, wading through the main channel at the low water of a spring tide. Timing carefully to be back before the water rushes in again. Every time Joanne and I go out, the trust deepens. The alignment between us becomes sharper. My skills improve and the joy continues. The healing is profound. I start to time my monthly cycle with the tides and the moon.

By April next year I will leave it all. My husband, my

home, the horses and Penny, my dog. These are the things I love more than anything in the world. But already the finger of the Great Mother is beckoning me to another path. One that will bring me into an understanding of the deeper mysteries, of wombs and women, horses and healing.

I am moving through the room. Backwards. Guided in this session by a dance therapist in whom I have complete trust.[1] I have come to her in desperation. My throat is raw and burning. I am very sick. Step by step I explore the pain, the monthly reality of womb's blood not fertile. At each point of intense emotion, tears flow and sobs burst out of me. She says, 'Stop now.' And so I do. She continues to guide me: 'Explore it, what is it?' I sob: 'The sea, the sea! How could I live without the sea at the side of my house? To bathe in each summer morning. Or to watch the red and pink and gold of summer sunsets on the ocean, out to the west behind us.'

Images of my life pour forth as I continue to move through the room. I see us out on the sea on a boat. An early morning fishing trip. A balmy morning in May. Leaving the house just after dawn when the sun has risen and the sky is pure and clear. Pink light stretching across the top of the mountains in the east. Not a sound, save the gentle hum of the engine as it pushes the boat through the channel. Moments of looking at the man I love. The profile of his face. Intent in concentration. A strong arm, tanned with the sun, holding the rudder. Guiding us out to the open sea. An hour later, the chug-chug-chug of the engine gliding back through the calm waters, as we return with mackerel caught for breakfast.

I see us of an autumn evening. We are gathered around our large oval table. A dinner party with friends: artists, poets, teachers and fish-farmers. We all pause to admire the views out of the window to the strand beyond. Faces animated, conversation is heated and alive. Enjoying the food. Simple, wholesome food. Roast of kid goat and fresh vegetables from the garden.

I see myself setting off for a walk with my dog, Penny. Out across the wall at the back of the house and along the pebbled beach that leads over to the ruin of Killaspugbrone Church. She runs round me jumping as I play a game with her. We walk on, out beyond, to the edge of the ocean and find a spot to sit and watch the sunset on a clear spring evening in April.

As I move more and more into these images, the silent scream, buried in my sick throat, comes forth, so clearly, in words now:

> *The dance to live.*
> *To give life.*
> *To keep love alive.*

I see a picture of a 'tree of life'. On the ground surrounding it are flowers of all colours. Rich with summer's fresh scent. Bright, soft, beautiful. I say:

> *The tree is my relationship.*
> *The flowers are my children.*

I draw a picture of the tree and the flowers around it. I weep with both the joy and the sadness. This is an impossible reality to know and affirm. However, at the end of this session with this skilled therapist, I breathe more easily. My throat has cleared of its burning rawness.

Summer 1990

It is the mountains in Sligo that resonate with my name. A cry of grief is transforming itself into a song. I start to go there and climb, pushing up and up. As supervisor of an environmental arts project, it is my job to find safe paths up the mountains. Based in an old school at Calry, under Keelogyboy, I bring the work team of thirty-three people out to connect with the land, its alignments and its power. Over a whole year we create outdoor theatre, art installations and, in the forest nearby, a performance in nature for children. We finish with a spectacular show of lights on Knocknarea. During the course of this project, I climb all the mountains in the heart of County Sligo.

To every mountain I go and find my way to the top. I go to find answers. *What is happening to me? What has become of our life together?* The land's song echoes my song: Keelogyboy, Kesh, Killary; Slieve Daeane, Benbulben, Carrowkeel; Knocknarea, Knockalongy and Truskmore. They all speak to me and call my spirit outwards. My vision is clearing and now I see. I will belong to this land always. Through love and dedication to my work. Through whatever that journey will be, it is mine to take. In all of these skills, I will train and learn: drama and dance and their transforming power. The healing essence of creativity and theatre.

The mythical Dé Danann have reached me, awakened me and called me. Their Goddesses swirl through my dreams, filling me up with the eternal symbols of Celtic power: Danu the Swan, Morrígan the Raven, Brigid the Goddess of fire. They are, they say, the spirit teachers who will guide my path into this vast wilderness of ancient female domain. Back into the heart of Ireland with them I will go and dream the myths on.

The same year I spend many Sunday mornings in conversation with my husband. For hours we sit around our kitchen table and tease out possibilities, explore options. The range is lit and warm, sunlight often in the yard. Stopping to make another cup of tea or a second breakfast with coffee. A precious and blessed time. Digging for truths beyond us and asking for assistance: *What is the right way forward here?*

For the highest good of two people who manage, in spite of everything to the contrary, to hold the love between them.

The decision is made. I am going to leave all this. I say *Yes* to the call. Without any maps, I will make my own. I will walk the path along the raw edges of myth and soul in Ireland. And someday, somehow, I will come forth and sing the song of the feminine light, through me, in me, and in the mountains around me, from the awakened soul of this precious land.

After this momentous decision, I return to the mountains where soft rain envelops me and mingles with the tears on my face. A vision opens up. A host of women emerge from the hills. *Grandmothers of Birth and Death*, singing a song of deep, deep loss. It echoes my own great loss at the choice to go. Listen to the chorus of the Grandmothers! Their voices are mournful with a sadness that reaches to eternity. They come forth with their strength and blessing:

We'll hold the spirit of your future self, many years from now.
Come back to us and tell us when this work is done.

In April 1991, this work begins as I find myself with nine women friends, angels all, helping me to decorate and transform a neglected two-storey gate lodge. It is situated in a townland called Ballygrania at the edge of the Markree Castle estate in Colloney. About nine miles from Strandhill. Although in very bad repair, this house is solidly built and beautifully designed. We will turn it into a comfortable home of peace and woman-warmth.

One Saturday we do mighty work together. Sometimes silent and absorbed in a task. Other times chatting with humour and laughter. Then back into the silence. Each piece of work finished brings me closer to the reality of living here. The blue range is the main feature in the sitting room. A woman who lives in a gate lodge across the road will tell me that the first resident of my house ordered the light-blue range because she loved the colour of it. It is clean and shining now and ready to burn a good fire. The walls in all the rooms are painted. The windows are washed and their frames glossed.

In the middle of the afternoon picnic hampers of food are brought in. We open a bottle of wine to toast a new life.

Something starts to crack in me. A sense of heart-breaking loss has come in through the door and is tangibly present. I leave the company and go outside to walk. A wet, dull, afternoon. Over the field to the right is a wide, deep-flowing river. The Unshin. It goes under a beautifully curved stone bridge. Out in front are green fields, the parklands of the large estate. Above the tree line you can see the tops of the Bricklieve Mountains in the distance. The woodlands close in on me and I miss the sea already. My heart is breaking as I realise I will not see the setting of the sun on the ocean. The colour of the orange sun stretching out along the sea and disappearing below the horizon is my symbol of happiness, home and eternal love. Now I will be living without all of this.

Two weeks later, on a bright Sunday afternoon, I drive my car over there to live. Orange berberis is blooming brightly in many of the gardens along the road, under Knocknarea, all the way from Strandhill to Ballygrania.

CHAPTER FIVE
Meeting Macha

Dance with the trees
In the moon's pure light.
Dance beside the river.
You can make it,
You can make it,
You can make it new.
Animal spirits come in the night,
Come to keep you company.
Wolves and bears, deer and frogs.
Open the door and let them in
For they will be your kin.

Spring 1991, Sligo

I am thirty-three years old. I have stepped from my home at the sea's edge to live alone in this small two-storey house. In the soft, gentle terrain of green countryside, on the edge of woodlands on one side, and beside the River Unshin on the other, I open up to a place of deep surrender.

In these first few weeks I experience a loneliness so deep that words could never describe it. There is a power, however, that comes through from way beyond the pain. It is like the golden light of a women's choir, singing in harmony and, like the voices of angels, it lifts me up and up. To heaven almost. It comes sometimes at dawn as I wake to another day. The sound of it fills my whole body with a healing light of pure gold.

Spirit helpers come at dawn,
Bringing ancient wisdom.
Go outside and greet them.
Receive what they will bring to you
For they will help you, too.
Listen, listen, listen.
Listen to their song.
One, two, three, four,
Listen to their song.

Held safely in the embrace of the Great Mother, this has become a quiet sanctuary for a new life. I have opened my heart to an eternal presence of the ancient Sacred Feminine.

It is the Celtic Goddess Danu and her love that holds me here. She is the magic mother of the sparkling dawn, showing me the hidden faces of herself. She is in the sound of the crows in the second chimney that wake me up each morning. I find her in the beauty of the trees as I walk through the woods, collecting firewood to bring back and chop for burning in the blue range. In the river outside my house, she is in the swans gliding down the slow, deep-moving mass of water. Every day the swans are there. In the summer, I will slip into these brown waters each morning to bathe.

One rainy morning in June, I sit at my table looking out at the trees, all in full leaf now, soft and green. I am writing the weekly logbook for the arts project I supervise. With the patter of falling rain there is a chant coming in. I stop and listen:

Pouring rain outside your window
Hopping off the paths.
You will make it,
You will make it,
You will make it through.
Oak trees, beech trees, chestnut, too.
They will whisper,
You can make it,
You can make it through.

Autumn 1991

An artist companion and I make sculptures of stone on the top of Truskmore Mountain in the north of Sligo. Each stone is lifted and placed into a form. A double spiral emerges. It is a prayer that eternal love may come again. A trip to Slieve League in Donegal. Two whole days climbing at the sea cliffs. Leaning now, exhausted, on a turf pile at the side of the road. Smiling face flushed. Love the rugged, raw feel of Donegal. Create a pact with the land for new to come.

Early autumn. Leaves of red and rust made into pictures. Art, beauty, nature. The pain is gone. Moving on. A 'river' made of dead wood is crafted from the bottom of a decaying tree in Hazelwood forest. I work intently for hours on this piece. My companion, the artist, takes photos of it. I am standing on a stone out in the water on the edge of Lough Gill. 'Dancing on the waters of life,' I say. He answers: 'That could be the title of your book.'

Moments of transcendence with the land are all prayers for the future. I am building inner reserves for the years to come, drawing as much strength as possible from the elements, the beauty, and the mythic magic of Sligo.

I go to Dublin each week to study Jungian psychology. A world of archetypes and myth opens itself to me, taking me into the altered spaces, and the slow-moving world of spirits and dreams.

The *Night-Sea Journey*, the Jungians call it. The descent of the soul into the depths of the psyche. The journey seems natural and right. A soul that has been breached with grief is already open for this passage. I attend therapy every week, searching for the lost feminine in the depth of shadows.

A map is given to me in the patterns coming forth. Images from myths come into my dreams. Celtic and Greek symbols. Triple spirals and light coming out of the mountains. Persephone and her pomegranate. Psyche and Eros; the candle wax lighting the faces unknown. The kind attention of my therapist and her dedication to the Goddess is a blessing beyond measure.

More disturbing pictures come from deeper places, sorting themselves into patterns and themes. Wizened old women trapped under lakes. Young women held captive in dungeons. Babies smashed along the rocks. In all of it, the destructive male and female within me are torturing my own soul, trying to release the past and forge something new. Over the months of winter into spring, I see the changes in the dream patterns. Healing permeates my cells.

I study the structures of Greek myths and stories. The characters, the journeys, and the presence of their gods: Odysseus and Athena, Dionysus and Hermes. The tricksters are messengers of the divine. They occupy liminal spaces with me and, by disrupting and creating mischief, they help me to travel across the thresholds to other worlds. Understanding the meaning within all of this, I find answers to my questions about the power of myth for healing. And, as the wheels of the seasons turn, I am opening the pathways to a new life.

Spring 1992

It is in early spring of 1992 that I meet Macha for the first time. I am sitting at my table by the window looking out on the green pastures beyond. The first touches of warmth can be felt in the air. The large trees, branches still bare, grace the parkland in front and the slow-moving River Unshin is over to the right beyond the grass. It has been flowing past me all winter, deep and dark. In the far distance, south of my window, I can just see one Cairn on the top of Carrowkeel. Then the blue-grey corner of the mountain disappears behind the line of trees at the river.

I am writing an essay on the Great Mother Goddess. *Who was she?* Sumerian, Celtic, Greek and Roman. My words take shape on the page. Female, soul, earth, womb. Inanna, Brigid, Demeter, Diana. I stop to let the next piece of writing shape itself within me. I slow down my thoughts to get to the very essence of what it is I need to say: *In Greek mythology, Artemis is the Goddess of the wild.* She touches me deeply. With all the animal and spirit helpers around me now in the invisible realms, I resonate strongly with her. I pause to look out the window.

In my mind's eye I see Artemis, Goddess of the animals and the hunt. She is in the woods of Greece. As I narrow my eyes, this image shifts back to the Irish countryside. When I focus deeply and ease my breathing I can hear the sound of a horse's hooves beating out a rhythm in the distance. The sound is coming closer and closer. The air is poised and still.

A vision unfolds in my mind's eye: I hear a knock on the door. I open it. When I look outside, I see a woman there, standing tall and proud. She has just jumped off a horse, sweat on her face. Her long dark hair is wet and tangled. Wearing a gown that is dark grey with threads of silver through it, she has a queenly presence about her. I am aware of the shimmering, alive spirit of her whole being. With a wild look in her eyes, she is filled with impatient power and she speaks without delay: 'I am Macha, the one who runs with the horses. I am of the Danann people from across the waves. A daughter of the ocean, I am the wild feminine spirit here in the land of Ireland. Go and find my story and put that into your work. Walk with me now and I'll teach you the wisdom your soul is yearning to find. The ancient truth of female knowledge.'

I stand up and look at her, eye to eye. I am shaken at how real she feels to me. My reverie suddenly filled with this power. No words. Finally breaking the silence, I say to her: 'Yes, I will go with you.'

In all my years of work in myth and outdoor theatre with the stories of the Tuatha Dé Danann and the other Celtic Mother Goddesses, this is my first encounter with Macha, the Horse Goddess of Ulster.

After this meeting with Macha, whatever part of her has come into me this spring, my power is restored and I never look back again.

> *A dream of silver spider webs*
> *Holds me like the full moon light*
> *That glistens as I look out my window.*
> *The dark silent river is lit up*
> *With a stream of shimmering moonlight.*

I wake again in the morning. My heart and soul are at

peace. I am bathed in the pure light of a baby reborn.

A call from my friend Tess, the editor of the *Aisling* magazine on Inis Mór, invites me to send in my Jungian essay on the *Great Mother Goddess*.[1] It will be published in the next edition.

Inspired with the rich depths of feminine spirit in me now, new forms of work are bursting forth. Along with a colleague, I design a workshop for St Angela's College called *The Great Mother*. A sizeable group of women and two men attend. Using dance, voice, drumming and song, we move everyone through a process of awakening the Goddess within. A beautiful day of colour, creativity and celebration.

At the end of it, I have a healing glow in my belly, deeper than I have ever experienced before. Thus begins exciting new connections across Ireland with like-minded women who are dedicated to the return of the divine feminine.

Summer 1992

As spring moves into summer, I plant a garden in the form of a mandala, shaping the ridges in squares around the centre. As I plant the seeds at the new moon, I call on the power of the Mother Goddess to bless everything that will grow here. I call myself a daughter of the moon. I am a young maiden, connecting with the power of cosmic fertility, in me and in the land around me. Linked to female transformation, and drawing on the life force from beyond me, I have enjoyed, so much, this year of new birth.

In July, I go to Kilkenny to attend the *Lover's Journey*, a week-long workshop directed by Paul Rebillot. A born theatre director with a generous heart, Paul brings great creativity, colour and laughter to all of his work. On the first night we dance. I am in my element to be back on my feet and out of the psychology books. My beloved dance and drama combine now with the work of transforming the shadow. Everything of the familiar comes back to me as the skill of gestalt therapy opens newly to me.[2]

Most of all I love its artistry. The giving of symbolic form to the process through lyrical abstraction, ceremony and ritual. The beauty of this work touches my core and at the end of it, my whole body and soul are glowing. It has been a magnificent week of exploring the opposites of female and male archetypes and the healing of these within. And even more is the joy that, in this man, who is a master of transformation within mythic structures, I have found the teacher with whom I can train to do the work I was born to do.

Three weeks later, one of my nine angel women is driving me to Shannon for a plane bound for New York, en route to San Francisco. I clutch in my hands the card from another of the nine women, carefully written to send me off: *Don't forget the flowers in San Fran.* The music of *A Woman's Heart* CD[3] sings out from the speakers. I look out the car window at the passing scenery and wonder: *How on earth did this happen so quickly?* In a moment of universal opening so great, a whole new world has called me. This trip is a manifestation of so many things, that it would make you believe in miracles.

On a scorching hot Saturday morning, I arrive at a retreat centre in California to be greeted by Paul Rebillot and the three women of the faculty of the North American School of Gestalt and Experiential Teaching.[4] All are seated at a table for the late morning brunch. Having answered their astonished questions as to how I got here at all, I turn to greet a woman with long grey hair and sparkling blue eyes. She is wearing a flowing, pink and purple dress. She is grounded and earthed as no-one I have ever met. Carol Proudfoot-Edgar, shamanic practitioner and Bear Medicine woman, opens her arms to me. We embrace as though we are sisters who have been long apart. Her wide, slow smile takes me in: *The young woman who has trekked here from Ireland.* Over the next eight years I will work closely with her and train in the practice of shamanism, held in the teachings of Bear Medicine.[5]

I fly back to Ireland three weeks later, greatly changed by the experience. I hardly recognise the places around me in Ballygrania. The energy in Sligo that has supported and nourished me for so long is closing down fast. There is an urgency to move. The call now is to go and meet the wild feminine. To Inis Mór. To Macha.

The Saturday following my return from California, I am stumbling up the road from the boat in Kilronan, heading for An Charraig, a house at Eochaill on Inis Mór Island. The raw barrenness of the grey rock cuts into me. *I cannot live here*, I say to myself, *not after the fertile, green loveliness of Ballygrania.* I spend an hour talking with my friend Tess. An expert herself in Jungian dream analysis, she helps me to tease out the themes in my dreams that point to my moving on. I go for a swim later that morning. My face is softened with tears and my heart is filled with gratitude for all of it. I am welcome here. I make the decision to leave Ballygrania and come and live with Tess and Dara at An Charraig and share their lifestyle in Celtic Spirituality.[6] This friendship and the island itself will hold all of what I need, as I commit to the four years of my training course in the US.

And so on this September morning as I say *Yes* to the next stage of this journey, a deep relationship with the people and the land of this island, begins. Inis Mór is the largest of those three mystical islands that sit out beyond the waves in Galway Bay.

In the late summer, shortly after my visit to Inis Mór, I gather with my nine women friends to celebrate the harvest from the garden. I look at the basket of vegetables that I have brought to this feast, all picked from my 'moon garden'. Orange carrots with fresh green tops. Purple beetroot and green bunches of lettuce and herbs. The fermenting process that took place in the four bell jars that sat beside my blue range and bubbled all through the winter has produced a rich Elderberry wine.

I look around at these women, sprawled on cushions and a sofa. All of us, in the bright colours of summer clothes, sit and talk, laugh and cry, drinking this potent red wine. It is a year and a half since we decorated the gate lodge together. We have had several gatherings in the time since. Women soul sisters, we have shared so much here in Sligo over the past ten years. We know how to cook, enjoy good food and talk. We have worked many times together doing artistic productions with dance, theatre and drama. Changing times, unknown futures, yet linked eternally with the Grandmothers of this land. I trust this connection of love and respect will hold firm for many years to come.

A week later, I clear out my lovely house in Ballygrania, gathering everything of value to put into storage. A big fire beside the river burns the discarded remnants of my life here in the countryside. Eighteen months of a beautiful woman's sanctuary. Recalling it all and in a quiet place of peace, I say my goodbyes to the house in the woods. I sing my gratitude to the land. The trees, birds, animal spirits and the river listen to my song. Later, standing at the fire with two of my women friends, we are enveloped in a starry night. We can see the waning moon as we go and sit under the chestnut tree. For the longest time, we watch the light of the fire's embers being carried up, high into the sky.

CHAPTER SIX
Beyond the Waves

Mystical mythical magic of the west
Take me and make me new.
Spirits of the Tuatha Dé Danann
Open the door to your places
Across the waves.
Allow the forces of sun and rain,
Wind and hail,
To play upon me
And strengthen the elemental power within me.
Teach me to endure
So that I may find that part of me
That yearns to know
The ancient spiritual teachings
Of the land of Ireland.

Autumn 1992, Inis Mór

To try and reclaim the lost treasures in the soul of the land is a lifetime's journey. I begin this next stage of it when I step onto the ferry to Inis Mór one evening in early October with only a rucksack of clothes, a black bag with my quilt and a fiddle strapped across my back. It is an exquisite evening. The daylight is fading and the skies are clearing. I am leaning on the railings of the boat as it pulls out of Ros a Mhíl. I watch one of my angel women on the shore. Six weeks now since we drove to Shannon together. She is sending me off, waving fervently, and, as the boat speeds out to the ocean, she disappears from sight and I am left alone with my thoughts. Moving across the waves, I watch the fiery red sun setting in the west, out in the ocean beyond us as far as the eye can see. The beginning of joy comes at last.

I walk over the deck to the railings on the other side and I see a full moon rising up against the darkening sky in the east. Its silver radiance is a comfort in the journey ahead. As I hold myself in this exquisite balance of sunset and moonrise, I know that from this moment on the work of reclaiming the feminine in the land and soul of Ireland will begin in earnest, and it will be a challenging path. All across the western world, women are claiming their connection to the Great Holy Mother. A newly awakening feminine spirit is calling us all back home.

Inis Mór is a place set apart. It is awesome in its stark beauty. To live here all year round, you must honour the wild forces or they will destroy you. The people here know that. It is a quiet knowing that survives beneath the hustle and bustle of tending to the tourists as they come and go.

All of this is part of the mystery of Inis Mór. Go there and step off the boat with only what you carry on your back and spend a few days out on the land. Then you might know that you are meeting with an unfathomable spiritual power in a place of deep, ancient, archetypal truth. The challenge here is one of survival. Of body and soul and spirit. On a grey rock of land that will cut you to the core and remake you anew. Year after year, your truth, and the truth of the land. Slowly revealed.

Over the next few days I am caught in a whirlwind of activity. RTÉ television are making a film about Celtic Spirituality here on Inis Mór.[1] I meet storytellers, guides, musicians and pilgrims, all of whom have chosen to live here in search of a spiritual way of life. I am folded easily into this group of people: *You can help with the conducting of this ritual – Will you play the fiddle here? – Perhaps you could say a few words about why you came here to live?*

A week later, on a day of bright sun and intermittent showers, I am walking down the road, heading out towards the cliffs at Dun Aengus. Autumn rainbows grace the sky. My hair, grown long over the past two years, is tied up in a scarf and I am wearing a new navy, wax raincoat and hiking boots. Essential clothing for this lifestyle. Dun Aengus is that massive stone fort of semi-circular walls hanging above the swirling waves of the Atlantic Ocean. Today, after climbing up the coastal path to it, I find a quiet place to sit on a flat rock, not too close to the edge. Perched high above the turquoise waters, I hear the sea pounding against the cliffs. Seagulls are swirling below as I take the pure, clean power of this magnificent place into me. I ask the spirits: *For what have I come here?*

After an hour in quiet meditation and chanting, my head is cleared of any doubts. I have grasped what my purpose here will be: I will forge a new way through and find a spirituality of the earth connected to the feminine light and to the female body being sacred. Up on this high cliff at Dun Aengus, I find myself aligned with my whole spirit's destiny. In the coming months, it is to this place

I will come each week to take stock of all. Here is where I will find clarity, vision and vital power. This practice, of going to the spirits of the land for answers, will become a way of life for me.

The Celtic spiritual way of life connects with the feminine in its honouring of cycles and seasons, tides and moons, land and sea. All are an integral part of the flow of each day. Within the rhythm of spiritual life there is a respect for silence. You can be with others and stay within yourself.

My soul is thriving on this balance. A frugal life with the satisfaction of a daily rhythm. Physical work blends with intellectual pursuits. Mornings of dance or writing for *Aisling* magazine. Afternoons of gardening or walking to the sea. I learn to do things slowly and with grace. All practical work becomes a meditation, a prayer, in response to whatever is needed. Writing, gardening, baking bread. Waves of comfort, belonging, simplicity.

When the day is finished, we sit around the fire and quietly read. I hold a shiny, black hardback book in my hands. It is Clarissa Pinkola Estés' *Women Who Run With the Wolves*.[2] A treasure brought back from California. Studying her words each evening, her stories are giving me the map for the next stage of my journey to find the wild girl-soul within me.

Within the bond of friendship in this household, I find myself a part of an ancient awakening of forces. A pact is made and an ancient blessing given, expanding us all into a new way forward. The tension I hold between the Christian aspects of Celtic Spirituality and my exploration of the divine feminine, is a superb creative force that calls me forth to engage in a daily dance of discovery and challenge. And yet I know, it is exactly the right measure of tension to temper my spirituality into a durable form that will not crumble in the face of shadow.

I spend a lot of time outdoors. Walking up narrow paths

flanked with high stone walls. A shower of rain can come suddenly. Pulling on waterproofs before you get soaked. Sheltering behind a wall. Shivering with cold.

My body becomes lean in the harsher climate, yet this island is bringing forth a strengthening of spirit and a deepening of personal power that would be numbed by the comforts of everyday existence elsewhere. I cycle everywhere. Over to the lodge to dance. Come back to cook or eat the lunch. Join with others to go to the garden for the afternoon.

I am exhilarated with the vital power of this island. The shifting clouds, the showers of rain. What I love about it, is the changing light in each hour of the day. The land is bleak and barren. Yet the play of light makes it so beautiful.

I begin to see that Macha is the Wild Mother here. Every day in the raw vitality of wind and rain and sea I find her. Like her wild spirit, all here is dynamic and powerful. Restless and free. Seeping right in to my bones. I move through autumn and winter beckoned by this force. Every day I see more of the power of the feminine in the sea, the waves, and the rock. Stoats run along stone walls. A wild place, safe for small animals.

Two mornings a week I go to the lodge where there is a workshop room in which I can dance. Through the dance I find the power to keep my spirit going. Strengthen me, bless me, heal me. This is the song that draws out my courage to face the challenges of this new life.

In the afternoons, I go down to the field at the shore to help with the work. A day in November, digging and gathering potatoes. The fresh afternoon air of a coming winter season is chill on the face and yet exhilarating. The physical work stretches our bodies. A visceral sense of the season changing. A woman from New Zealand digs beside me. I stop and lean on a spade to watch her. She is wearing a big yellow raincoat and, as she straightens herself up, she turns to me, smiling. We are both red-faced and content.

Connecting here for a few weeks before she will move on with her journey of visiting Ireland.

On many mornings through the autumn I walk down about a half mile to the rocky beach below the house. Some mornings I sit in silence on a rock and simply notice the shifts in the light and energy. I love the spray of the sea on my face and in my hair. On other days I sing to the Wild Mother in the waves. A 'thank you' for everything that is given here:

Wild Mother, carry me, a child I will always be,
Wild Mother, carry me down to the sea.[3]

The smell of the seaweed is strong as piles of it are decaying on the shore. I watch as little birds feed in it. The sea faces north, out to Connemara. It is often rough with waves and other times, gentle. Always changing, light and shade.

As the wheel of the year turns through the seasons, I begin to know the feel of the shifting energies. Like an ancestral memory, these energies come up from the depth of a landscape that still holds the power of ancient magic. In the Celtic tradition the New Year begins at Samhain, 1 November.[4] The Celts knew that all life first begins in the darkness of the womb and they honoured this. A seed is planted and allowed to grow in the silence of winter.

I will learn over the years here on Inis Mór that the mystery of Samhain is connected with the descent of the soul into the darkness. On the island, the energy of this transition into winter is intense. The veils get thin here like no other place I have ever been. The presence of spirits, ancestors and elemental energy is tangible. It is seven weeks to the winter solstice and during this period, if you are attuned to the energy, you will feel the drawing down of your soul into the shadow of dark and strange worlds.

It is the end of October. There is a grey mist stillness

holding me. I surrender to this unknown stream of energy that is drawing me across the veil and making strange distortions to my sense of reality. I have a period and blood is flowing clearly and red. My belly is in terrible pain and I need to find relief. Terror is gripping my insides. Slowly building up pressure. The emotional pain is deeper than I have ever felt.

It is night-time and I go outside to find a place to be alone. My senses are keen. I know where to tread on the rough path as it twists and turns and takes me down steadily to the sea. On the shore I step carefully over each stone finding my way to the water's edge. Out in the darkest night I have never felt closer to the Wild Mother who is guiding me on this journey. Here at the water's edge, I stand up, raise my hands and shout out loud into the dead of night. I watch a few lights on the coast beyond as the echo of the night takes my cries of anguish.

Finally, finding some peace and the strength to trust this, I make my way back up the track and go to bed. Tears roll down my cheeks like a grief that will never end. I grieve my mate, my children, my home. The pain is so raw. My womb, ovaries and hips are on fire. I am frightened. I lie awake and wonder: *Is this amount of searing pain okay?*

The following morning I awake to rain dripping down. Dreary, grey, miserable. I go to meditation and the quiet time is useful. I stay on alone afterwards. I look at the altar and I hear my voice say to God: *Please help me to find a way to heal the part of me that bleeds with pain.*

After breakfast, I go outside and make my way down to the sea again. More tears are pouring down my cheeks. I let them flow and when I get to the Wild Mother's beach, I hear a voice that answers my prayer: *They have their own story, the women in your family line who have gone before you. Greater than your pain. Your blood is shed and the pain released for those women who never had a voice for their womanhood.* I understand a broader message also: *You are being shown this because you have asked for answers and have come here to find them. Your womb is a vessel of transformation. You give birth to new energetic forms when you are not giving birth to children.*

As I listen to this voice, the physical pain ceases and with that, the fear goes. Ease and healing spread through my whole body. Transcendence. I return to the house and, with a beautiful sense of peace, drift into sleep.

The experience in these few days around Samhain is the beginning of my learning how to pass across the veils of time. I understand somehow that the womb provides a passage to the spirit world. In this very intense menstruation, I travelled beyond myself and into the collective soul of women. I have an image of a road with a 'No Entry' sign. It is obstructed with briars, thick and impenetrable. Passages to the spirit world through the womb have been blocked for centuries.

CHAPTER SEVEN
Transformation

'Don't run from me,' Macha says,
'You've run long enough.
I want your song and your tears and your pain.
It helps me to know I am real.'
The sun looks different
If you've been into the cave.
It's the gaps, those bits you don't see,
That really make the picture
When you come back out
Into the light.
What you remember
Is the balanced light of darkness.

January 1993, Inis Mór

In the early days of the New Year there are special moments at dusk when you can see the stretch in the light. A brightness in the west that lifts your spirits and helps you to face into another year with strength and vigour. You watch a moment. White waves crash at dusk. It is still winter but the light is different. You breathe and you know you are through. The Samhain descent is complete. New growth has started and your soul is renewed. You will hold this new growth in stillness through January, until Brigid's Day at Imbolc on 1 February when you emerge fully to the next season of spring.[1] You will be much strengthened by the safe passage through winter's dark.

Most of January this year is harsh and cold, with winds battering at the doors and windows. Heavy storms at sea continue every week. One day at lunchtime, I am standing outside the front door, taking in deep breaths to freshen my head after a morning of writing. It is the day before my birthday. This evening, in the Celtic tradition of celebrating the eve of a special day, the people who live here will light candles on a cake for me. Folk will come to dinner. They will all wish me well for turning thirty-five.

Today is softer, brighter,
A warmer day.
Connemara looks fresh and beautiful,
With the Twelve Bens, crystal clear.
Snow on top.
Bright green sea and white waves,
The ocean is cold
But also clear.

I have begun to write a series of articles on *Celtic Myth and Healing*. In these articles, I trace the origins of myth in

Ireland and how we lost our soul with the Romanisation of our native spirituality.

I continue to dance on Tuesday and Thursday mornings and take the themes for the writing into movement. I am drawing up from my body the wisdom that has been taking root all winter. Teasing out the truths I want to speak about. Just below the surface. Intuited. Not yet clear. The Dé Danann mythic ones are speaking to me. I am searching for the balance of female and male and I want to integrate my experiences of the old Celtic soul and the energies of the land with the light of a dignified Christ, in his truest form, before the Romans distorted his image.

A quaternity of divine beings emerges: Brigid, Macha, Lugh and Cernunnos. A wheel of opposites. Female and male. Dark and light. Earth and sun. Soul and spirit. Wild and cultured. Brigid of light and spirit. Macha is her wild sister riding a horse across the land. Lugh the Sun God, with his shining Danann sword, emerges as the forerunner of Christ, who too is a solar God, with his 'word', the sword of truth. And finally Cernunnos, the man of the earth, with the healing snakes entwined around him. He is the one who is cleansing and transforming the pollution in the soul of the land.

Opening the door for 'new' to come in, I listen to Sharon Shannon's music. It is a link with an ancient life force. I sense a new pathway being forged through women's music and song that will help to awaken the old soul. This pathway is feminine, gentle, joyful and light. It is like the soft magic of the Burren landscape and the mythic life force of Galway blended together. Vibrant and moving, magically dancing. Connecting me deeper and deeper into the past of Ireland, it also points the way forward:

The old soul begins to sing again
Of ancient wisdom and sacred sites,

Amen, I say to you, Wild Mother,
I am yours.

By the end of January, I have a great sense of renewal and three articles written. One is for this month's magazine, Imbolc in February. The second will be published at Bealtaine in May, and the last one will be in the Lúghnasa edition in August.[2]

The following morning I go up to Dun Eochaill. It is a day of hail showers and intermittent sunshine. As it is not far from the house, I often go to Dun Eochaill for a breath of fresh air. Sometimes I sit on the top of the walls and meditate in the sunshine. Other times I dance on the grass inside the stone fort. It is a place, I find, that strengthens the power of women.

Today, I circle around inside the high stone walls invoking Macha to hear me. This Macha who comes today is huge. Towering over me, she is challenging and elemental, raw and powerful. I am scared to death of the full, visceral presence of her. Once I get over the shock of it, she speaks to me about the blood mysteries, telling me that Dun Eochaill is a womb space and she has a few important lessons to convey to me such as: 'Your mother gave birth to you in pain. She suffered severe blood loss and almost died herself.'

Up here at this Dun with Macha, I realise today, with incredible clarity, how much my mother had suffered to bring me into the world. I know the story of my birth, but within the power of Eochaill today, I grasp a bigger part of it, that my mother had given me the greatest gift possible – the gift of life.

I begin to really understand the sacredness of giving birth and the tremendous energy a mother gives to bring in a baby's soul from the other world to this one, as well as the physical exertion and pain. It is the most incredible act of spiritual passage that exists in our world. A flash, a memory:

A baby girl is fighting for her life.
Snow outside, heavy snow.
Blood on the sheets and the floor.
Transfusions wheeled in on trolleys.
A cry is let out in the room.
Was it her cry or mine?
'At least the baby is alive,'
I hear them say.
A daddy goes home to the other children,
'Your mummy is alright now.'

A mother whose own mother is long dead.
Behind all of this, is the aching, bleak emptiness
Of a town in Northern Ireland.
Lisburn, at the end of the 1950s.
A flash of this darkness,
Carries in the memory of the newly born infant.

The story goes that after ten days, I was brought back into the hospital for an operation to remove 'poison' from my throat. I was there for six weeks until St Patrick's Day. My mother had said to me: 'You were in an oxygen tent. I came to see you every day and a woman we knew from down the road was a nurse in the Lagan Valley. She kept an eye on you all the time you were in there.'

Standing in silent awe as the deeper truth of it dawns on me, I look over at Macha, tears soft on my cheeks. She nods slowly, as if confirming the story. Her face is tender as she regards me now. I hold eye contact with her for a long time and finally I sing, thanking my mother for giving birth to me. As Macha sings with me, the song spreads out from this ancient stone fort for mothers and daughters everywhere:

I will hold your daughters in my arms.

As I leave Eochaill, two crows fly overhead. They appear again at the bottom of the lane and follow me all the way back to the house. I stand at the door and watch them fly off across the sky. Inside, we have some fresh kid goat, newly killed and ready for the freezer. No-one else is here today. I fry up the goat's heart and liver and eat it for lunch. A fitting communion to honour this memory of my own mother, and the encounter with Macha.

Several weeks later, in March 1993, at the time of the spring equinox, I come face-to-face with Macha's deepest wound as she expresses the rage of what has been done to women in Ireland by the powers of the early Church and colonisation:

'You show me your rage, Macha, at the time of the equinox storms. A cold grey day in March, on the barren cliffs of Inis Mór Island. You show me how the Church fathers did systematically destroy you and all you stand for. You show me what they, and later the English Cromwellians, did to crush the power of you in the earth, stone and rock under our feet, on this wild, free, elemental place. This beautiful island.

'You show me how they crushed your natural bond with your babies and children. Ripping apart all of your instincts, courage and deep womb wisdom. And then they shredded the dress you were wearing to add further shame to an already defiled body.

'You speak in hushed tones: "The story was so, all over the land of Ireland. It is visible here on this barren island because the veils are thin between this world and the next. And the memories in the land so raw and hidden, seen only by sensitive souls forced to meet their own raw and challenged places."

'And even then, Macha, you show me your tears as you weep for everything you have lost. All knowledge stolen from you. You ask that somehow there would be those of us who would stand for you now and reclaim all of who you were before they came to hunt you out of those birthing, loving, mothering, living, wild places. You ask that we might find a way to free our wombs from the legacy of what was done to our natural wisdom. To find a way for our daughters to know you. And not just to know you, but to live your ways, your passion, and power. In their bodies, free from shame. Oh, Macha ...

'And even more, you ask that when the rage is spent there would come a time for forgiveness, when we will bring forth the joy and the pure beauty of womanhood into the world again. And you ask that then, in our hearts, we would call ourselves home.'

Macha's rage and the rage I felt in the land brought my rage to the surface. Macha was glad to see the rage in me, a balance necessary, she says.

In the weeks following this, I dance it all out of me. An onslaught of darkness and fury against the Catholic Church's denigration of my body and spirit and the feminine truth of all women. And when I dig down into the heart of it, I find a seven-year-old girl deeply betrayed in body and soul. Here is where the poison starts. In her primary spiritual awakening time, as she makes her first Holy Communion, into the fragile vessel of a little girl's divine self, we pour in images of a male God.

The forces of nature hold me. The Wild Mothers hold me. Macha holds me. From the deepest places in my soul I call on all of them to carry me through to the light again. And when I do come out of it a very interesting thing happens. I see that the light of Christ is a good thing for a little girl's soul. What the Church's communion lacks is balance.

Macha speaks to this:

'And what is wrong with it is not so much that they put Christ in, but they take the Goddess out of it. So a girl's physical body is separated from her soul's light. The real poison of this does not kick in until she is fourteen and has become a young woman. Babies and young children, girls and boys, belong to the Goddess and not to the Church. The balance of power will change when women get through the rage and out the other end. The rage is the engine that drives this all to some kind of integration. In your cells. In your bones.

'The truth, stripped of all illusions and delusions. The rage is the power that will shift this lie out of the depth of your core. Begin this now, for it will take many years to come to completion.'

In my dreams I track the presence of a fiery gypsy woman. She is whole in herself, dark and mysterious, sexually free from anything defined by Church or man. At a deeper level, I claim back the sacramental grace of both female and male archetypes. Macha, Brigid, Cernunnos and Lugh, and the healed light of Christ. Through dance, I transform them all to a new place. With a potent balance of 'yin' and 'yang' in my own soul and spirit, this is *my* communion. The one the Jungians call *The Sacred Marriage Within the Self.*[3]

When I do finally emerge, clear and empowered, I take my little seven-year-old 'self' and I bring her down to the sea. I hold her and sing her back into her body, putting warmth into her bones and love into her heart. I rock her until her tears have stopped and promise never to betray her again by pushing her into boxes that were meant for men. She, in all of us, is the girl who will grow into the woman who will carry into the world, the teachings of female spiritual truth.

During the summer of 1993, I create music. I track my spiritual girl. Finding my song, her song. She is free now to allow the brightness of her essence to shine forth. With tremendous gratitude and celebration for all that has been achieved, I travel home to Lisburn to visit my folks.

Seeking my soul I find it here,
Reclaiming a link with my mother.
I see the softness of her spirit,
Her kindness, love and warmth,
In nurture and good food.
Sitting in the lovely sanctuary
Of her garden,
I see beautiful flowers.
Pink foxgloves,
Pansies of purple, blue and gentle white.
Tall pink lavatera
Rising upwards,
And lupins of all colours.
I envelop myself in this warmth.
My body is soft and nourished
Amidst these colours.
I draw a foxglove
Onto a white page.
Heart of my heart,
Healed so much
In one short year.

CHAPTER EIGHT
Emerging New

Will you put into the well
Of the collective soul of women,
Images of Healed Feminine light?

If you do,
The well will become rich
With new power.

Future generations of women,
Can draw on this source
To nourish their world.

August 1993, California

I leave Ireland to go to California to begin my training in Experiential Teaching with Paul Rebillot. We are based in a retreat centre near to Monterey. I love the warmth of the sun and the ease of the lifestyle here. It is in such contrast with the elemental rawness of Inis Mór. My heart softens after a year of battering in the wild.

'Come in from the cold, Daughter, we want to see you,' I hear a member of the group say to me. I weep with love and thanks. Intimacy restored. Connected. Over the three weeks in America, I make great progress with my journey to birth the wild woman in me.

A power wells up in me.
I am a great bear rising upwards, afraid of nothing.
Growling, standing, filled with rage,
I raise my hands to the heavens and let out a roar.
I am one with all.
Long in gestation, something is coming out of me.
A birth.
I am a woman complete in myself.
I have, within me, the wisdom of the wild,
An understanding of the blood mysteries
And the secrets of womanhood.
A deep, powerful sexuality is integrated
With an expansive, total spirituality.
I am connected to all women,
To all men through their feminine,
And to all of nature and the cosmos.
I am the flow of life in underground rivers.
I am ready to teach the journey I have made.

In the autumn, after my return from America, I make a commitment to stay on the island for the four years it will take to finish my training. Every year now, I will do this journey across the Atlantic in January and September and stay there for almost a month at a time.

Over the autumn and winter I do several workshops on themes from Celtic mythology. As well as using the skills I am learning on my training, these creative mythic structures are guided from beyond me by the spirits of the island and the ancient Celtic energies now activated in my soul. They provide inspiration, ideas and clarity that help to shape these journeys into safe structures for transformation.

I move into my own house just before Christmas. Standing up on a rise overlooking the low road that runs along the sheltered coast of Inis Mór, Cregg Cottage is a modernised old homestead. It is a place of ease and comfort and, with the same yellow-painted doors and windows as my house in Ballygrania, I have come home again to my own sanctuary. The white walls inside are bright and there is a cosy fire that warms my heart. I thrive in the joy, beauty and abundance of this new home. There is a beach below me and I go there and walk each morning before the day begins. Sometimes at dusk, I go down to the water's edge and dance along the shore, singing songs from Sean Tyrrell and KD Lang.

In mid-January 1994, just before my birthday, I go again to the US and continue learning the art of facilitating gestalt therapy. With a further week of the 'Hero's Journey', we learn about the artistic process, and the skills necessary to design a structure for teaching mythic journeys of transformation.

In February, when I return again from the three weeks in California, two women who are teaching an organic gardening course on the island come to live with me and share my house. My garden is flourishing with their help.

It is the season of Bealtaine and on the first weekend in May 1994, women have come to Inis Mór from Sligo, Dublin, Galway and Cork to a workshop entitled *Celtic Goddesses, Women and Soul*.[1] As soon as they get off the boat, they are challenged by the sheer elemental force of this place. Each one is asked by the spirit of the Wild Mother: *For what have you come?*

> *Ancient Mother, we hear you calling,*
> *Ancient Mother, we hear your song.*
> *Brigid, Danu, Macha and Morrígan.*
> *Brigid, Danu, Macha and Morrígan.*[2]

On Saturday morning after tea and coffee and some chat in the kitchen, twelve women and myself enter the workshop room. A large circle is marked out in stones with an altar on the floor in the middle. Each stone has a coloured candle beside it, a circle of cushions surrounds the stones. It is a 'Wheel of Life', designed to hold the energies of the Celtic Goddesses. There are four drums placed around the circle at each of the four directions. Every woman is invited to ask herself: *At which place on this circle shall I sit? East with Danu, south with Brigid, west with Macha or north with Morrígan?*

In the singing that follows the introductions, voices rise and fall in harmony. Nourishing and gentle. Magical to listen to. With soft drumming, we call in Danu to join us in our dance. And, in a light breeze of air, sparkling like the stillness of the dawn, you can feel the moment this Great Mother enters the room.

When we call Brigid, she comes in with the strength of fire. The upbeat tempo of her spirit creates a dance of fun and laughter. Singing and alive, we close the morning.

Return again, return again,
Return to the land of your soul ... [3]

After lunch, the resistance from the awakening cells in our bodies creates a dip in the energy. A desire to sleep. We lie on the floor and do a visualisation to evoke Macha into our midst. Wild and free, she comes in from the sea today and calls us up and out of the heaviness. See the waves wash over the women as they lie on the floor, taking her power into them as they rest. Women rise up to move as Macha's power moves through them. Watch the soul dance in a dance with her.

As the resistance is released in this dance, we glimpse the rage within these vibrating cells. But Macha's life force takes us out of the shadows lurking beneath the skin. Always this is her way. First, into the resistance and inertia, and then slowly to the light. Something new is trying to be born.

The resistance to the Goddess Morrígan is so great, that we lie in complete stillness, unable to move. Her stark challenge takes us all by surprise. We have to earn the entrance of Morrígan into our midst. She is saying: 'Go into the darkness of the deep earth to connect with me.'

Once in alignment with her, however, she calls us into a powerful dance that finishes with a still posture of her dark, embodied beauty. By mid-afternoon, all four of these Celtic Goddesses are tangibly present in the room.

We are the walking breath,
We are the spirit of the earth.
We are alive and walking,
Where we are is beautiful.[4]

On Sunday morning, each woman draws a mandala of her experience of the Goddesses. The gentle presence of Danu and her sparkling green magic contrasts with the wild, raw force of Macha. Distinguish Brigid's creativity – which is active, outward and moving – from Morrígan's poised form that guides us through the dark.

Connected by the elements and the seasons, a collective mandala of integrated feminine emerges from all of the drawings: east, south, west and north. Spring, summer, autumn and winter. Thirteen women move forward in mythic time. It is a beginning. A map to show the way. Souls evolving.

When you do this work, the shadow of the feminine also comes up. Touching on the wounds. Asks for healing. Resists healing. Creates pain. We know, therefore, as the wheel of the seasons turns, the journey to Macha's light will be a long one.

After the weekend I realise the power of what has been given. A great gift. This Mandala of the Celtic Goddesses is a vessel that will hold many journeys of transformation for women seeking a new form of spirituality and healing.[5] It is not a return to an Earth Goddess way of being, but the forging of a new constellation of energy that will hold the images and patterns of the future.

I give thanks to all of the women who attended the weekend. And to the four Goddesses who graced the room with their presence. For Brigid and Morrígan who direct the crafting of the work through light and dark. For Danu and Macha who nourish our woman souls in their new becoming.

September 1994, California

I return again to California for the second year of the myth and gestalt training. I love the moment of arriving into JFK airport in New York and feeling enveloped with that warm, damp air. America. The waiting time and then the ease of a half-empty evening flight to San Francisco, arriving in around 9.00pm. The warm, dry air here caresses your face as you come out of the terminal and look for a minibus to take you to the downtown hotel. People in shorts and bright summer clothes all about you. Breathe. So glad to get a break from Ireland.

After three weeks of the Rebillot training at the Mount Madonna Centre near to Monterey, I fly south to Los Angeles and out to Jacumba, a retreat centre close to the San Bernardino Mountains. The hot sun of the Californian High Desert beats down on us. Carol Proudfoot-Edgar is the medicine woman with the laughing, blue eyes. She carries the power of the Lakota people in her blood and the sparkling mischievous humour of the Irish in her soul. In her tutelage she tracks with 'Bear Mother' to teach us the skills of shamanic practice.[6] In a Bear circle together, we embark on a deep reclaiming of the feminine in our very cells. Communicating now with the spirits of plants, stones and crystals, we learn how to ask for their healing medicine. In the afternoons I go out over the dry desert hills with a few of the women, now 'Bear Sisters' to me, and play music for the land and the ancestors here.

Under a full moon shifting in and out of high clouds, we dance all night to the sound of the mother drum. Looking out through the fringes of a leather mask, reality is shifting in and out of Otherworlds. The women dancing around me are changing from Bears to women and back to Bears. The drum continues on and on, a steady beat held under the desert sky. On the fiddle, playing a dervish dance into the night, with the pulsing energy of spirit power in all of us, I hear them say: 'Come on, Fiddling Bear, play us another tune from Ireland.'

Enriched, I return to Inis Mór for the winter of 1994. Glad to be back at Cregg Cottage again, I walk to the beach each morning.

All winter I continue to craft the Celtic workshops, putting into practice the new skills from both training courses: Bear Medicine Shamanism and Mythic Drama and Gestalt. People from all over Ireland travel across to the island, stay in B&Bs, and participate in these journeys with the Celtic Goddesses, myths and stories. New places of transformed soul are forged within all of us.

Summer 1995, Inis Mór

One afternoon in May, on the boat trip back to the island, I meet PJ O'Flaherty, a fine musician and songwriter. He lives on the island and, along with his wife Grace, runs two restaurants. He has heard that I play the fiddle and asks me to be a part of a recording of the island's musical heritage.[7] It is a pivotal moment. A light goes on. I agree. After this recording, which I thoroughly enjoy, music becomes my life for the whole summer. Ease comes in like a river of gold. I shed all the challenges that come from doing so much transformation work, year in, year out. Playing gigs four nights a week with several of the musicians on the island, I have become, simply, a 'musician'.

During this glorious hot summer of sunshine and outdoor living, many folk and family come to visit me. Joy streams in and something quite beautiful is manifesting around me. It is a whole new relationship with music, with the island and the people here. In this magical shift of focus, I have learned that the playing of music is core to who I am.

During this summer, my mother, Mary, comes for a week's holiday. I go into Galway to meet her off the train from Dublin where she stayed with my brother and his family. My dad, Michael, would have loved the ease of the Aran Islands and the mighty music sessions. But as he is no longer well enough to make this kind of a journey, my mother has travelled alone.

A few days later, in a bright floral skirt and blue tee-shirt, Mary is standing outside on the grass in front of Cregg Cottage. It is a warm evening and I can see that she is relaxed and happy. As she looks out towards the sea and the peaks of the Twelve Bens in the distance, I can see her strong profile, tanned with the summer's sun. My mother was reared in the wild places of north Antrim. Those heather moors, wild seas and rugged headlands of Fair Head, Murlough and Torr. It gave her a strong spirit and a healthy body. I see all of this reflected in her this evening. She loves the wildness of Aran. I want to wrap her in my arms and take her home. Up there, to her roots.

The next day she and I are out early and getting off a bus at the foot of Dun Aengus. Still young for her seventy-nine years, she is easily able to walk up to the old stone fort. A photograph will show us both up here, enjoying the smell of the sea, and the serene morning beauty of this exhilarating place.

At the musicians' table in the pub, my mother is sitting beside me. There are four of us here with instruments, playing tunes and singing songs. The place is packed with summer visitors, dressed in tee-shirts and shorts or skirts and colourful tops. The atmosphere is overflowing with summer's goodwill and happy smiles. I finish a tune and Mary nudges me and rattles the ice in her empty glass. In my memory, her Ballycastle kinfolk liked to drink whiskey when in a pub together. I smile, knowing that in many years from now, these will be the moments of her that I will always remember.

Summer 1996, Inis Mór

Another year on and I have spent the winter in Galway city, working as a gestalt therapist. I have missed the wildness of Inis Mór and I return for the summer as the resident musician of the Dún Aonghasa restaurant. Travelling out each week and staying at the staff house from Wednesdays to Sundays, I thrive again in this rhythm of life.

On the beach below Cregg Cottage, I sit and ponder the four years here. With the years of transformation in my bones, my body and soul are deeply healed. The two training courses in Mythic Gestalt Drama and Bear Medicine Shamanism are both almost finished and my own work with these, in an Irish context, is finely honed. In everything, there is a sense of completion. There have been several visitors from Belfast at the music sessions this season. I enjoy their banter and humour, and the call of the Northern soul gets stronger and stronger in me. I am yearning to go home. It is 1996 and a pivotal time as Ulster moves into a new chapter of peace.

The spirits are asking for healing work alongside of this process: 'Will you go?'

I write letters to everyone I know in the North of Ireland: 'Will my work be received?'

I hear the drumbeat of Ulster, throbbing in my veins, calling me home:

Return, Daughter, return.
'Fill aríst a 'níon, fill aríst ...'
It was before Cú Chulainn's time
That she was banished,
She, they call Macha.
'Go, woman, go.'
We, the warriors of Ulster,
Want no weakness of women
In our midst.
'Go, woman, go.'

She left her curse on them,
You will see it in their faces,
The fear that some day she will come back.
Return, Daughter, return.
'Fill aríst a 'níon, fill aríst ...'
I hear Macha's voice in the shadows
Calling me back to Ulster.
'Fill aríst a 'níon, fill aríst ...'

PART III

Transforming the Wounds

CHAPTER NINE
Ardun House

A tunnel of trees up a lane.
Magical.
A house made ready for guests.
Glowing.
A hammock swaying between the trees.
Serene.
Horses moving around in a paddock.
Beauty.
A porch filled with sunlight and flowers.
Inviting.

September 1998, Glenties

It is two years since I left Galway and the Aran Islands and moved to Donegal. I am standing in the yard of Ardun House, a healing centre on seventy acres of land, owned by Margit, the woman with the magic touch.

Situated in a valley in west Donegal, close to Glenties town and surrounded by sheltered hillsides and soft green land, this land is a perfect place to do healing work with women. The River Owenea flows through the valley, and in front of Carnaween, the highest peak in the Bluestack Mountains, there are two peaks in the distance. These two hold the power of the dawn as the sun is rising over the valley from Ardun. They give a sense of perspective as they lift the spirit up and out at any moment during a weekend workshop. I love this work in Donegal and relaxing here as I take in the view, I recall the past few years that have taken me to this moment.

In December 1996, I moved from Galway to Killybegs in Donegal. On Brigid's Day, 1 February 1997, I did the final piece of work to complete the gestalt and experiential training with Paul Rebillot. Twenty people travelled from many places around Ireland to Glencolmcille for this workshop which I called: *Birthing That Which is New Within*. We crafted a womb of willow withies with four doorways, each marked with a white quartz stone for strength and support. We 'gave birth' to clay sculptures, crafted in the morning and representing the 'new' coming into our lives. Brigid, as spiritual midwife, filled the day with her light. It marked the beginning of my work up here in the northern regions of Ireland.

By May 1997, Macha was urging me to move closer to the six counties. I moved to Muff in June, a border town close to Derry city. There were new projects taking shape and the impact of the Peace Process was just beginning. It was an exciting time. Attitudes in the North were changing. New hope was pushing us out beyond the years of war. Seeds for peace were being sown and they were taking root in people's hearts and minds. We could glimpse a brighter future.

I was welcomed with warmth. A coming home, refreshingly new.

Since then it has been slow, painstaking work. Emotionally demanding. Souls empty of warmth. An echo of trauma in people's voices. A drumbeat of fear in the distance. Damage so deep. How would you ever get to the bottom of it? And where do I find Macha in this wounded, betrayed, angry culture? It was like going through a doorway and everything I had carefully forged fell away. I left aside the beauty and mythic magic that I had been working with on Inis Mór: *Get real. Myths aren't going to heal us up here.*

Today, I am glad to be here at Ardun House in the hills of Glenties. As I watch the horses in a small paddock beside the stables, it is a breath of fresh air to be working out in the wilds again.

My intention today is to find a place on the land for the Celtic Mandala and create a space for ceremony as I prepare for a group of eight women who will arrive this evening to Ardun House for a weekend workshop. At the autumn equinox, two weeks from now, a group of American women on a Celtic Goddess pilgrimage will join these eight women for a day's celebration here at Ardun House.

I head out past the horse barn along the bottom of the lane and find the path up and over the wall. Within a tangle of trees at the edge of the field there is a small river. I push into the bushes and follow this stream up the hill, picking my steps over and back across it to find a way through the undergrowth. Up a good way, I push through the briars and overgrowth and come out into a large field. I take time to stand at the side of the field and look out. The air is warm on my face although I can smell autumn in it. I breathe in deeply and start to walk slowly across the field, noticing that the land is fairly dry. I look out at the hills across the valley. It is facing south and we will get the sun in the daytime. I am asking: *Will this field do for ceremony?*

I walk to the middle of the field and pace out the size of a circle we will use for the Celtic Mandala. It is the same form that we first discovered that year on Inis Mór at Bealtaine, with each Great Mother Goddess at a compass direction and linked with each of the four elements. Although I have used it several times since 1994 for workshop weekends, this is the first time to bring it to an outdoor setting.

I call in the power of the spirits of the land to support the work that will come, inviting the Grandmothers, the animals, trees, and waters, minerals and stone, to gather with us here to assist the work. As a soft wind shimmers, the feel of the air changes and the sun bursts through with a beam of light. I sense the spirits of the land coming to meet me. I find four large stones and put one in each direction: east, south, west and north, thus marking out the places around the circle for each Great Mother.

I gather up my things and walk back down to the house. I find Margit laying out the table for our lunch. I see that she has soup on the stove and bread cut ready to go into a basket. I put the bread in the basket and bring it out to the table. I sit quietly as I wait for her to join me with the bowls of soup. The whole house has a sparkle about it, the result of her careful preparation for the women coming this evening.

After eating, I take my tea outside and sit on a bench in the warmth. It is a pleasant afternoon and I am happy to rest in the quiet peace here at Ardun. The past few years of working in the North of Ireland has been a challenging time.

The weekend begins as the eight women from Ireland start to arrive. By supper time there are nine of us gathered around the table.

As we start our meal, there is an excitement in the air. Some of these women I know and others I am meeting for the first time. We introduce ourselves and they chat about their journeys to get here. This is a magical moment. There is a flow of grace that arises and all the preparations in the house, the food, the workshop space and in the land, start to sing in unison. I breathe deeply, relax and surrender to the flow.

At the table I hear different voices blend together as these women talk excitedly to each other. Accents from Roscommon, Germany, Meath and England blend with others from the North, Galway, America and Dublin. An ease in this group is immediately evident.

We open our circle after the meal and move into the work. The women have brought with them precious objects, scarves and cushions and place them carefully in front of them as each shares the story of what has brought them here this weekend.

The following day they go off on their separate ways in search of a place on the land that will be a sanctuary space. Led by their intuition, they follow paths around the seventy acres of Margit's land. Somewhere out there, they will stop and say: *Yes, here is my place.* Defining a boundary for shelter by tying scarves and coloured ribbons onto tree branches or walls, each woman will decorate her place and imbue it with her own healing intention. They will take the whole afternoon for this quiet crafting. It is Brigid's energy that assists us with the creativity and inspiration for this.

While the women are out on the land, I craft four large prayer sticks to put up in the field at the Celtic Mandala. Taking straight cuts of wood, sycamore and hazel, of some six feet in length, and using bright-coloured wool and feathers, beads and small shells, I decorate each in turn for one of the four Great Mothers. Brigid first, in the yellow and reds of fire, and then Macha, with a blue for water with silver threads running through it. Danu is in silver-grey and white for air and for her place as mother of the Tuatha Dé Danann. Finally, for Morrígan and her element of earth, I pick out wool in black for death, golden yellow for rebirth, and weave these colours around her stick. I prop each one against the barn door and when finished, I stand back and survey the power that is now infused into each of them.

Later in the day, we all go together to visit the special places that the women have created. These have become places of power where we all can walk into, sit on cushions on the ground in quiet contemplation and hear the stories of each women's theme for her sanctuary space.

We end our day at the ceremony field. We put the prayer sticks into the earth at each of the four directions and, together, sing in the spirits of the Celtic Mother Goddesses. Thus blessed, the Mandala now holds the power of Danu in the east, Brigid in the south, Macha in the west and Morrígan in the north.

With this weekend's work finished, we close our circle. Taking in those few things that might spoil in the rain, we leave the shelters intact. Margit and I stand in the yard to wave goodbye as the women drive their cars out of the lane and head off along the valley where they will find their roads back to homes and families.

At the moment of departure of a weekend retreat where deep work has taken place, there is a subtle light that flows in and leaves its own gratitude. It is as if the soul of the land is shimmering. Trees and flowers radiate their essence and even the red paint on the front door looks brighter.

CHAPTER TEN
Immram

An Immram is a spiritual journey.
Across the threshold to another world.
The intersection of myth and ordinary time,
Creates an experience of
Altered times and places.
It is a hero's journey of death and rebirth.

September 1998, West of Ireland

Tell them the truth
For the lies are tired now.
The lies about who women are.
The lies are dying
With the old world.
And the healing, created
By many women
Who have chosen to walk
The shadows of the past,
Has changed the soul
Of womanhood today
At deep and influential,
Mythic and archetypal levels.
These women are changing
The cellular memories
Passed down over hundreds of years
In female lines,
Sticky with fear and tarnished with shame.
Diminished thus
By our own mothers' frightened hearts,
How could we have taken our place
Of trust in the world?
In the rising up of these truths,
Tentatively being spoken now,
Women of courage today
Are risking the terror that is real
And has been real in the world,
For what has been done in centuries past,
Is not to be taken lightly.
Women have blazed the trail such that
The spirit of the wild feminine
Can now come home
And take residence

In women's bodies and souls,
And be passed without fear
Along female birthing lines.
This is Macha in her most powerful self.
Thank you, Macha,
We are coming home,
Women of Ulster, Ireland, and across the world.

It is three weeks since I was in Glenties with the eight women who live in Ireland. Having spent a week on the Aran Islands and Connemara with a travelling group of women from the US, I am now sitting at the front of the bus to give directions to Noreen our driver, an astute woman from Kerry who organises our logistics. On this sunny Saturday morning we are travelling through Mayo and heading north to Donegal.

In February 1998, two American women, Carlotta and Suzanne, had invited me to join with them as a guide and help with the design of a Celtic Goddess pilgrimage along the west coast of Ireland. They wanted to go to wilder places such as Inis Mór, Sligo and Donegal to find the spiritual roots of the feminine in the land.[1]

Carlotta, whose grandmother taught her the magic of the Irish soul as she was growing up in Boston, has a deep love of the land here and an in-born resonance with the Celtic feminine. Suzanne's strong mother kept her connected with her Irish roots and to the female spirit of the land. She has an exceptional skill for translating a vision into practical reality. Noreen, from Tralee in Kerry, is the fourth member of our team. She has the deep goddess power of Munster embedded in her whole being.

A pilgrimage journey is a very different experience to a workshop or retreat. Here, we are in motion from place to place. Each location is carefully chosen for its ability to help us to connect with the inherent power of a Celtic

Goddess. Travelling by bus, there is a constant movement in time and space. When we stop, we are exposed to the elements, the land and to the people and culture around us. All of these experiences become a part of the journey. On a pilgrimage, you cannot control or predict what will happen. You surrender to the story unfolding. The land speaks to you. Guides you. Shows you signs.

Our leadership team is strong for this type of a trip. Our design has clear intentions and a seamless structure. The logistics are carefully planned, scheduled and timed. Then we let go and trust the unfolding of all we encounter.

On this trip today I am sitting beside a woman from Ohio who is dressed in a bright-yellow tee-shirt that matches the mood of the day. She is talking excitedly about everything she is discovering on this trip. She recalls the boat ride from Doolin in County Clare across to the island of Inis Mór. High waves and the boat rolling over and back. All our bags were lifted onto benches to prevent them being soaked by the seawater sloshing all over the deck. Women were sitting in rain gear, their faces anxious, their fingers white with cold, clutching tightly to the old metal rails, rusted and repainted. A few hours after the boat trip, the sun was shining at Dun Aengus. We lay at the edge of the cliffs and looked down on swirling blue seas with white waves dashing up against the rocks below us. Exhilarating and breathtaking.

At the guesthouse in the evening, we told the story of Macha running the race against the horses of the King and giving birth to her twins at the end of the track. The crowd ignoring her cries for help. All of the images were vivid and struck a chord with these women. Awakened by the challenging, inherent power on Inis Mór, there was a resonance with Macha's vulnerability. Safe that night though, in the cosy sitting room and watching the fire burn in the grate in front of us.

I tell the woman in the yellow tee-shirt about my years on Inis Mór. How I was moved to tears last week with the joy of bringing a group to Dun Eochaill. It had been a chilly morning with rain pouring down as we sang together to greet the wild spirit of the Horse Goddess of the land. I told her I was in awe to find myself back there with a group of women, remembering my words with Macha in 1993: *I will hold your daughters in my arms.*

From the seats behind us, there is a lot of laughter from all of the women on the bus. We have just emerged from three days in Connemara in a challenging battle with Morrígan. As the Celtic Goddess of 'death and transformation', she will strip you to the bone before she lets you see your light. Everyone is feeling the relief to be through that encounter.

I keep my eyes pinned to the road. Checking the signposts for our route. Having moved up to the small seat at the door beside Noreen, I give her directions at a junction and stay there to take in the scenery of Mayo. Croagh Patrick is on our right as we wind our way towards Westport. I glance back down the bus to check the mood, make eye contact with Carlotta and Suzanne and confirm that all is well. A quiet has descended now and we are rolling along the road with ease.

The shift from Mayo into Sligo and coming north towards the mountains has a wild and rugged feel. We stop at Knocknarea, the sacred hill in County Sligo, and some of us climb up to the stone Cairn at the top of the hill where Queen Medhbh is said to be buried. It was Medhbh, the warrior Queen of Connaught, who fought Cú Chulainn and the men of Ulster for the Brown Bull of Cooley. After that climb, there is a noticeable shift in the energy into the strong, passionate power of Medhbh. A Queen's warrior strength is called up in us now.

It is late in the day as we continue northwards to Donegal town and drive along the coast before swinging inland towards the town of Glenties. On the bus, I tell the story of Medhbh and that whilst all the Ulster warriors were struck down with the pangs of Macha, our Queen Medhbh was having a field day, smug in her expected defeat of these hopeless warriors of Ulster.[2] Then she realised that Cú Chulainn – whose father was Lugh the Sun God and, therefore, had divine Dé Danann blood in his veins – was unaffected by Macha's curse. An exceptional and ruthless warrior, he was taking Medhbh's men on single-handedly and winning every time.

We arrive early in the evening to the Highlands Hotel in Glenties. There is a heaviness here in the transition from the mystical west of Connaught to the earthed intensity of Ulster. I sense it every time I make this journey from Galway to Donegal. But then again there are shifts in energy that you can feel in every county of Ireland as you travel through it.

The maître d' shows us to a room beside the dining room. 'I thought you would like this,' she says. We look in and see a bright room with large windows letting in the evening sun. It is private and warm and daylight will stretch another hour or so. We file in and take seats at a long table that is laid for the sixteen of us. Beside us there are two long tables set ready for other guests.

We order our food and as we sit waiting to be served, a group of men starts to pour into the room chatting loudly and all carrying pints of beer. They fill up the tables beside us. There must be twenty of them all told, noisy and gregarious, their presence invades the whole place. A ripple of discontent passes along our table. We are irritated at this lack of privacy. It has been a long day travelling and we are all tired.

How could they think to put a group of women on a Goddess tour beside a gathering of rowdy men? But this is Donegal and I am sure the manageress thought we might like a little company.

At the same time, the men are craning their heads, curious to get a good look at us. They have tanned faces and are wearing bright-coloured tee-shirts. Chatting and joking, they are amused at being seated beside a group of women and are all ready to enjoy the evening.

As I listen to the strong accents and comments, it is clear that they are golfers on holiday from the North of Ireland. These men have an earthed strength and a comfortable presence about them. Their exchanges are quick and witty, and the banter has its own rhythm that is like a quickstep dance. They are assertive and loud, gesticulating with their hands and pointing at each other to emphasise a truth uttered and not to be debated. As I watch them I wonder: *What is it about Northerners that allows them to dominate a room when they come in?*

Our group has moved into a subdued silence, threatened by the unexpected force of this energy beside us. From the women at the bottom of the table, word passes along asking for an explanation that might make sense of this scenario on our mythic journey.

I pause in my watching. Stand back and ask: *What is deeper within this?* A dance of the trickster, listen to the tease: men from the North of Ireland ... therefore Ulstermen ... and the visit to Medhbh's mountain earlier today might explain some of it. *What has been activated in our ongoing myth? Are we, by any chance, being brought into the heart of Macha's story?*

And after some musing of these thoughts, I pass word back along the table: 'They are Ulstermen. Do you remember our story of Macha? We told it on Inis Mór in Galway. About the woman who ran the race against the horses of the King and gave birth to twins at the end of the racetrack? Well, we are in Donegal now, one of the original nine counties of Ulster. What we meet on our journey from here on in will be connected with the myths of the Ulster

Cycle. The memories of all of it will rise up to meet us in the land and people here.'

A ripple of understanding passes up from the women at the other end of the table. They nod their heads and glance over at the other tables to take in what men of Ulster, today, actually look like. Observing the regional differences in dress and appearance from those of Galway and Inis Mór. Tuning their ears to the accents. Satisfied with something that resonates with Macha and Medhbh, and the curse of the Ulstermen, everybody gives a sigh of relief. You can feel the ease in the atmosphere and more than a few smiles lighten the air.

As the food arrives, we get on with enjoying our meal. Queen Medhbh's energy has brought out the ravenous appetite in some of us and this might explain why several T-bone steaks were ordered. All of this is adding to the trickster mood of the whole evening.

Hey, Jude, don't make it bad,
Take a sad song and make it better,
Remember to let her into your heart,
Then you can start to make it better.[3]

Following our night at the Highlands Hotel, we are on the bus travelling out to Ardun House. We turn off at the Community Centre in Glenties and drive out the valley, east towards the peaks of the Bluestacks in front of us. There are a lot of twists and turns on this road for a medium-sized bus. We pass a row of low-roofed cottages and a big modern graveyard stretching up on the hill behind. Along the road a half-mile, we see an older graveyard on the right, quiet and reserved in itself and adorned with Celtic crosses. After this turn, the valley opens out wide in front and you can see the River Owenea meandering back and forth on the right. Several small lanes are signposted for fishing.

The bus continues another mile or so and just before another bend, I indicate to Noreen that we are close. We turn off the road, go through the gates and up along the wooded driveway with its tunnel of tall trees above us. We emerge into the sun-filled yard and can see the surrounding gardens, shrubs and trees. The two-storey white house is standing bright and clean, inviting us in.

The eight Irish women have all returned and, with shining faces and wide smiles, are there to greet us this morning. Their warmth envelops us immediately. As each American woman steps off the bus, she is welcomed with open arms as though she is a mother, sister or daughter returning to the shores of Ireland after a long exile.

After such a heartfelt welcome, we gather in small groups in the garden. Twenty-four women in all. Some are seated under trees. Others at the bench by the window. More sit in the glass porch filled with lovely flowers. We are graciously hosted by Margit. Drinking tea and coffee together, we chat for a long time.

On this Sunday morning in early autumn, a timelessness has crept in to be with us. There is a peace in the air and a sense of relief for the travelling women to be in a private place and not having to deal with any challenges of the road today. I see uncanny resemblances of the women in both groups. Facial expressions, colouring and hair, shape and sizes of bodies. All different ages, and yet it is as though many are kinfolk and always have been. The whole day becomes a sharing, a weaving together of the timeless experiences and wisdom of women across many cultures and generations.

After lunch, the women from Ireland speak about their sanctuary spaces on the land. What inspired them, what healing intention they held and why they chose the location to place it. The eight women then lead small groups out onto the land to visit their special places, where more stories will be shared and connections deepened.

At the end of the day we have all gathered on the hillside. Circled around the Celtic Mandala, we are watching a drama unfold. The women from America are taking turns to go into the centre and act out the story of their journey up the west coast. How they met Danu in County Clare. The rough and terrifying two-hour boat ride on a stormy sea from Doolin to Inis Mór. Macha welcoming us to her wild and beautiful island. The music night in the pub. Those harrowing days in Connemara with Morrígan's challenges, walking around with faces filled with confusion.

Finally, we see the dinner table in the Highlands Hotel and we hear some of the comments that were made by the golfers. We watch the women actors of Medhbh and Macha in conversation about the men of Ulster. Here in Donegal, it is Brigid who is guiding our creativity, with her sparkling energy and light. With faces raised to the late sunshine in the west, we give our thanks to all four of the Celtic Mother Goddesses and to Medhbh and her part of our journey as warrior Queen in the Ulster saga.

The beauty held in our midst at the end of this day is extraordinary. The warmth and sunshine of the autumn, after a very wet summer, has been a great blessing. It has soaked into all of our bones, giving us an unforgettable time of gentle healing, challenge, celebration and laughter.

Weaving of women, myth, land and soul.
Healing across Atlantic shores.

CHAPTER ELEVEN
Birth

Macha comes to the fore this year.
In a deep and urgent way, her story
Is looking for resolution
Of the wounding of women
Over centuries.
The spirits and the elements of the land
Will lend their power for
Transformation,
Cleansing, renewal and birth.
For the highest good of all,
We ask for their support to work onwards
With the myth of Macha.

September 1999, Glenties

When the time comes
For you to birth your baby,
The Grandmothers are standing at the door
Waiting for you,
Incense and water in their hands.
Rooms are cleaned and blessed,
The power of the Goddess is present.
Life and death are in the balance.
There is no illusion of this,
You knew it would be so,
They have you prepared.
With the help of a midwife,
Your baby comes forth
With the great joy that is hidden
Within the struggle.
The power of the divine
Pours through you.
Your body is healing already
With the presence of golden light
Brought forth at the same time
As the blood and the pain,
For these, too, you knew would come.
Water cleanses your body, washes the blood.
The wind takes your spirit upwards to release.
The earth and sky, moon and sun,
Receive your baby as a part of all.
The fire of love is chanted
By the dancing feet of the Grandmothers
Welcoming your baby's soul to this world.
It is the rhythm
Of dancing feet that brings the baby's soul
Fully into its little body.
The miracle of birth.

The baby's light moving downwards
Into the earth plane,
As its body is coming forth.
Euphoria that follows
The release of pain.
Light within your whole body.
The Grandmothers sing.
You listen as you sink into rest.
They will put a blanket around your shoulders
And sit with you in the quiet afterglow
Until you are well enough to eat.
Vulnerable exhaustion and deep peace.
In and out of dreams and waking states.
They will sing until your spirit is whole again.
Body and soul restored,
All returned.
You will be supported in the weeks that follow,
As your body recovers.
Your soul, too, is made whole again.
You will go forth intact when it is time.
They will tell you that giving birth to your baby
Is the most precious thing you will ever do.

I am on my way again to Ardun House in Glenties, preparing this year for four gatherings of women that will take place this autumn. I travel along the road with its familiar twists and turns, past the cottages, the new graveyard and the old one. The Owenea flows in the valley to my right as I turn the corners and measure the three miles out to Ardun. I look for the sign on my left and turn in. I am back in the yard now and stand and look out at the peaks of the Bluestacks. I go in to meet Margit, have tea and unpack.

Before I left for the weekend I had such severe menstrual cramps that I had to lie on the floor for over an hour and just breathe through the pain. It was as if I was giving birth.

It delayed me leaving and, in the quiet relief in my womb that came afterwards, I was able to hear Macha's words: 'This weekend is for me,' she is saying. 'This year's work will be about wombs and womb healing. It is about birth. You will see less of the wild Goddess spirit of me and more of the vulnerable woman.'

When I did finally leave Inishowen for the two and a half hour journey to Glenties, I was very tender, moving slowly with a vulnerable sense of relief. I am still withdrawn and quiet as I arrive at Margit's and decide to rest and wait until tomorrow morning before I go out onto the land.

On the bright and fresh day following, I am up in the ceremony field after breakfast. I mark out again the Celtic Mandala and remove the old prayer sticks from last year that, although now battered and broken, are still standing on the hillside. I begin to drum and ask for help for the weekend. Singing in the power of the spirits of the land, I send out my intentions for our workshop: to support the work that will come, inviting the Grandmothers, trees, waters and stone to gather with us here to assist us.

I drum and sing for a long time allowing the beings from the spirit world to gather around me. In the invisible realms, I see the Grandmothers gathering in the corner of the field. In front of me is Brigid. Macha is standing near to me. Animal spirits are coming in. I continue to drum and sing. A whole host of spirit presence is forming around me and the hill feels crowded. As I look into the valley in front of me there is a 'spirit river' with a lot of people in a boat. I am knowing it is the 'river of life', carrying the ancestors home. Many people are waving out at me as the boat passes. I begin to dance with the spirits that have gathered, slowly becoming one with them:

I am the Grandmother, hands in prayer.
Blessing, swaying, singing.
I am the wild horse,
Neighing, turning, galloping.
I am the ancestors on the boat,
Waving and feeling good to be seen.
I am the wolf on the hill, calling to the others.
I am the bears dancing,
The frogs hopping,
The snakes hissing.
I am the tree with birds swaying on my branches.
I am the eagle, swooping and circling around.
I am the Celtic Goddess, holding all.

I finish my song and come out of the altered place. Pondering the meaning of what I have seen, I stand for a while and let the power of it settle into my being. Breathe. Surrender. Trust. I hear Macha speak to me: 'The women are gathering to honour women's power, the land, and each other. Be with what comes, with your own stories and with the healing of the Grandmothers of this land. A birthing time. The grief held in this journey is a collective one.'

With some idea of what we might do for our weekend and quite shaken by these revelations, I leave the field and come down to the house for a second breakfast.

After eating, I take my tea outside and sit on a bench in the warmth. Reflecting on the content for the weekend and recalling this time last year when a group of women met here, and Brigid, in her sparkling light and creativity, emerged as the guide for that time. I realise that this year will be a much more intense journey with Macha. The signs are there and she has spoken. The preparations are in place. All I can do now is surrender.

Five Irish women gather in Glenties for the first weekend of the autumn. As we begin our circle, the rain is heavy outside and the room is filled with an unearthly stillness. The mood is sombre and dark. It seems as though we are walking through the land of the dead. As we drum, animal guides are called in from the spirit world. They will help to ground the work in a way that will safely hold its intensity. I see the 'river of life' with all of the ancestors waving to us, blending in with our stories as we gather in circle.

The following morning, two women of our group are out riding Margit's horses at dawn along the tracks of a lane. It runs along the valley beside the Owenea. On waking, I hear the clip-clop of the hooves. I open the sash window of my upstairs room and lean out to watch them come up the lane.

They dismount below and smile up at me. We exchange words of greeting. I watch them as they lead the two horses across the front of the house and down to the barn. I sigh with relief. It is a welcome sight after the heavy mood of the previous evening. I would give anything to have been with them on a trek along that river valley on such a beautiful morning.

We begin our work for the day. The five women create their own safe spaces on the land. With Macha's spirit guiding we are led into profound work: to do the healing and release of wounding, both of and beyond us. Ancestor women, who are now Grandmothers in the spirit world, welcome and witness this work. Their presence is felt around us. Gathered since last year and waiting for this, they heal and hold the rage and despair and bring us safely through the wounding. The land herself weeps tears.

Four new prayer sticks are crafted and placed in the ceremonial field in the four directions, one for each Celtic Great Mother. They stand with great dignity, this year taller and with stronger colours than before.

A photograph taken at the end of this day's work will show four women, standing in a line at the door of the barn. Strong and satisfied with the day's work, they look like women who can fight battles and win the war.

Sunday morning dawns bright and hopeful. Something has passed through the land. It is like the clearing that comes after rain. There is an urgency now to gather power in our group and assist the next piece with Macha. In a drama that follows in our morning circle, Macha runs the race again. Her hair wild and free, body heavy with child. She gives birth. This time there are women to hold her in the labour of delivering. And what she brings forth to the world is her healed self.

It was a quiet departure for the five women who left Ardun House on Sunday after lunch. Relieved and shaken, it will take a few weeks for that work to be integrated.

Two weeks later, I am travelling to Donegal with another group of American women on our Goddess pilgrimage. It was at Dun Eochaill again this year that we met Macha. The work with her was harrowing. Intense, with deep emotions. Transformation a core theme.

Having sailed from Inis Mór, we make our way north from Galway to Donegal. We stop in Sligo where some of us climb Knocknarea to Medhbh's Cairn. It is a slow pilgrimage up the mountain. We arrive on the top of the sacred hill, under an inky sky, heavy with rain. We huddle together for shelter in a hollowed-out place. Wind whips over us. There is an unearthly quiet. Something is coming to birth. We all feel it.

And here in front of us appears a vision of a young woman of sparkling aura. She is wearing a loose white dress tied at the waist with a red belt. Her calves are bare and on her feet are golden sandals with red ribbons that criss-cross up her ankles. Her light blonde hair is flowing long with a garland of blossom and leaves on it. Holding a golden branch in her hand, she is looking at us and speaks calmly: 'I am Niamh, a daughter of Macha. Look for me. You'll find me in the starry heavens.'

She smiles at us and the image of her fades back into the mist. But we feel a relief after this vision. Somehow the energy has lifted. We come off the Cairn and return down the hill, invigorated and refreshed. We are heading this year to a hotel in Glencolmcille to stay for the three nights over the equinox. The drive from Donegal town out to the coast seems endless. The forces pushing against us are strong and insistent. Raining and dark now, everything is mirroring the gathering challenges that are drawing us deeper into Macha's story.

Held up by traffic and wet roads, we arrive much later than expected. A woman with a Scottish accent is quizzing me about where we will eat in the next two days. *Is it her business?* I wonder. And as we eat our meal in the silence of deep exhaustion, I catch Noreen's eye. Thinking back to this time last year, I would be very glad to hear the good cheer of those Ulster golfers on a sunny evening in Glenties.

On the following day we are driving over the mountain to join the five Irish women at Ardun House. After tea and introductions, we gather in the workshop space. The energy of the whole group is tired, heavy and quiet. A strange atmosphere is present. After the drumming and the meditation, stories are shared and we listen with awe and with reverence. I can see the images of many things coming into the room. Centuries of women's stories; a collective pain. Energy like a dense cloud is building up.

'This is a lot for all of us to hold,' I am saying to Macha, and yet I hear her say to me: 'Rivers are coming in ... shimmering ... but heavy. Shapeshifting to other times. Two rivers of these cultures meeting. The room is dense with presences from beyond. Trust all. The Grandmothers of this land have asked for it and come to meet your women. Let it be.'

Later in the day, when the rain has eased, the whole group of nineteen makes its way up the hill to the Celtic

Mandala. Calling in the power of the Grandmothers to assist us, we enact a ceremony of 'birth' and 'release':

Slow motion, otherworldly.
A brighter evening as the sun shines in the west.
An opening in the sky.
Rivers of pale blue and soft rose-coloured light.
Grandmothers at the end of the valley are waving,
Arms reaching out to hold.
Souls fly upwards through a portal in the sky.
They take off with wings,
Floating in a light of blue and purple. Surreal.
They move through to another realm.

We finish our ceremony at dusk and stand looking up. The last rays of sunlight have faded and the clouds part. A single star appears, the Evening Star. In our mythic place, and hungry for relief from this day, we name her Niamh, the daughter of Macha whom we saw at Knocknarea. We believe that she might be the one to herald in the light of the Healed Feminine. With soft tears of joy and thanks, I am singing. I know a great passing of souls has taken place. A great cleansing in the land.

Back down the hill in Margit's dining room, we come in to find a delicious meal laid out for us. There are some smiles, a little laughter and great relief. But the mood is still quiet. Satisfied, we know we are through to something new.

The rage is spent, and,
As we transform this legacy
Of curse and shame
Passed down to us since Macha's time,
Forgiveness and joy may well still come,
And reside within us,
In the deepest place of our tender hearts.

PART IV
Lifting the Curse

CHAPTER TWELVE
Bear Medicine

I went to the cave
To look for Bear Mother
And learn the wisdom and
Healing ways of women.
She told me to find her
In the fire in my belly,
And then we would journey
To the stars.

October 1999, Glenties

If you were seven
And you joined with a group
Of other seven-year-olds,
And you had Grandmothers
To tell you stories
About being a girl,
You would learn
To trust the wise ways of women.
If the Grandmothers took you on walks
To rivers and streams
And taught you how to listen to their music
And then taught you how to sing back to them,
You would learn the language of water.
If they taught you to dance
The joy of being a girl,
You could move your body
To the beat of a drum outside in nature,
Freely across fields and grasses,
Greet the trees,
Dance with the wind.
Then you would learn always
To harmonise your pulse
With the rhythm of the earth.
When you turn thirteen
They will teach you about fire.
How to light a fire
That will release, cleanse and transform all.
How to keep the spark in your body alive,
And call fire into your belly.
And they will teach you
How to let the wind
Blow through you and around you.
You will learn how to use

The power of the air
To cleanse and uplift and strengthen your mind,
You, a girl who has become a woman.
The Grandmothers will bring you to the sea,
Where you will bathe your body
In the salt water of blue ocean.
Your newly forming body shape
Will be blessed
On its journey to womanhood.
With all of this you will learn about the elements,
To trust your own knowing and
To value your own instinct.
As you become a grown woman
You will watch the flow of blood each month
And know it is the moon
That pulls you,
As she pulls the tides in the everlasting
Ebb and flow of life.
Now the moon waters will move in you.
You will know how to call on their power to assist you
All the way through your bleeding and birthing years,
Into middle years and onto older places,
And you will never forget the way home.

Ten days after the pilgrimage, in October 1999, nine women from Arizona come to Ireland. They are part of a healing circle of trained medicine women, here to join we three Irish women, to help and support us in whatever way is called in our work of feminine healing. This group of twelve women in total are coming to spend nine days on a Bear Medicine retreat at Ardun House.

There is an unbroken thread in this gathering from the other retreats and pilgrimages over the past few years. All is in alignment now to push Macha's story through to completion before the new millennium. All twelve women here are folding into years and years of work together. We three Irish women have been here at Ardun before and so we bring in all the streams of energy from the previous groups of women.

I arrive the night before and the following morning I go up to the field to see what remains of our last gathering. It is ten days since we did the piece on 'Birth and Release'. I stand at the top corner and witness the ease that is here.

Suddenly I am startled out of my quiet sensing with the land to hear a ... *ssssushsssussssshing* ... sound. I turn around just in time to see five horses burst into the field through a gap in the hedge. They gallop down in front of me, restless and wild. These are Margit's horses and she has them out on the land this week. Two black mares, a white pony, a dappled grey mare and a chestnut gelding are doing a dance around the field. They rise up on hind legs, neighing loudly.

I stay still, relaxing into the delight of watching them. They canter right through the field and move in and around the circle of Celtic Mother Goddesses. They nose in gently at each prayer stick. When they are done, they stop to nuzzle each other in the middle and look over at me. It seems right that they are out on the land for this gathering. With a lot of work done here with Macha and women in the past two years, it is a joy to see this today.

That same evening, the twelve of us are gathered in the workshop space. We begin our circle with the moon in waning crescent. We ask: *What are we called here to do?* No-one knows as yet and as we walk the land and watch the horses running around the fields on the following morning, Thursday, we reflect on this question. Watching for the signs that will bring messages in from the spirit world.

On the hillside at the Celtic Mandala, we sing. The four prayer sticks hold the power of the previous gatherings. Listening to the messages from the spirits of the Mother Goddesses, we are welcomed here. There is a sense of release, a brightness. Cleansing rain is falling. I see a vision of children dancing and free. Stories are told. The healing spirit of Mother Bear joins with the power of Macha at the Celtic Mandala. Their common ground is the place of the west, where our power as women is in transformation, the instincts and the love and connection to animals.

This feeling of satisfaction and joy is so much a part of what I know as Bear Medicine. A laughing, childlike place of ease that is deeply rooted and bubbles up in the body. Many years of training and working in shamanism, where Bear Mother is a teacher in the spirit world, has taught me this.

Soft footprints on gentle earth.
The song is humming, humming.
The grass is singing, singing.
Our song is heard, heard.
A crow flies over,
Laughing, laughing.
The rain is falling, gently, softly.
On our faces, falling.

Within the practice of shamanism, the spirit of Mother Bear teaches us about restoring the power of the feminine. Bear Medicine strengthens women's bodies and souls. This teaching connects us with ancient circles of medicine women who, in the spirit world, still hold the wisdom of the indigenous healing arts. How do we use this strength and ease? First, be grounded deeply in the female body, with the senses restored and the instincts sharpened, power coming from the womb. Then, open the heart and mind to a place where deep and powerful spirit work can be done.

~

It is Friday morning, the third day of the retreat at Ardun House. Within our group there is conflict arising. Tension amongst us. Whispered words overheard. Misheard. Tipping the balance of trust. Mistrust. We sit and drum. There is shame surfacing in many of us. All kinds of shame are running through us all. Woman's shame, Catholic shame and Irish shame.

After lunch, we go our separate ways to seek assistance, clarity and power from the spirits of the land. I go up through the trees and follow the path of the little river on the eastern boundary. I criss-cross back and forth across it, looking for a clearing where I can sit beside the water. In a small glade of trees I stop and find a stone beside the stream. I take off my shoes and socks to bathe my feet in the water. I ask for release from the kind of shame that surfaces in women at the bleeding time of the month.

I look and see it is shallow here and there is gravel on the bottom. I take my clothes off and ease myself into the water. Freezing cold, I sit on the gravel. I pour water over my head, surrendering to that moment of contact. *River hold me, envelop me.* Fragile, vulnerable, calling to Macha *– be with me in this place.* I sing all the verses of the Wild Mother's song from Inis Mór.

As I sing, tears start to flow down my cheeks. Macha and Brigid have come in and are with me in this glade by the river. As I put my clothes back on, the song changes to another river song:

> *Oh, where are you now when we need you?*
> *What burns where the flame used to be?*
> *Are you gone like the snows of last winter?*
> *And will only our rivers run free?*[1]

Trusting the flow of spirit energy through me, I keep singing the words, as I remember them. Over and over:

> *I drink to the death of her manhood,*
> *Those men who would rather have died,*
> *Than to live in the cold chains of bondage,*
> *... still only our rivers run free.*[2]

As I am singing, I am weeping with grief and these words
are echoing in me:

> *The weakness of the Ulstermen,*
> *... the weakness of the men,*
> *... the death of our manhood.*

Today, I am on the edges of this pain. In our culture, in
myself. When I stand up to go, I cannot face going into the
open space of the field. I make my way back down to the
house. Finding no-one around, I boil the kettle for tea and
sit in an easy chair by the fire, alone and in silence.

In our circle this Friday evening the mood is subdued.
Many have spent the afternoon out on the land, walking
the hill or sitting to watch the horses. Some went across to
hike along the track at the Owenea river. Others crafted, a
few rested. All bring back the stories of their day.

We are in new territory. We look around at each other
hoping to find an answer to the question: *What are we
here to do?* The visiting women remind us again: they are
supporting us three Irish women towards healing whatever
is called for in Ireland. I bring the *rivers* song to the circle.

'What does it mean? Who sings it?' they ask. Another of
the Irish women answers the question. 'It is a song that the
Irish Republicans have taken as a signature song for the
nationalist cause. They see the land still in bondage and are
yearning for freedom.'

I sense us move slowly and silently to a new place of understanding about our call as healers. I open my heart to whatever it is that is wanting our attention. We ask the questions and begin to drum: *What do these themes mean to our work here? And what is needed of us for healing?*

The drumming is intense. I find myself singing a marching song. Strong, vibrant and insisting. I surrender to it and get up on my feet. In this otherworld place, I am brought to meet the spirits of three men of Ulster, long since dead. They were, in their life-time, members of the Orange Order. I converse with them and their words are poignant: 'We, too, carry shame, and would like to have healing done for wrongs of old. Will you bring this into your group?'

I see the sorrow in their eyes as they speak to me. It is Brigid's voice that I hear in the background: 'You women in this group are mature and seasoned now in all of your work. You are weaving part of the ongoing story of Ulster. You ask for peace. This is the next chapter. Surrender and trust. All of the rivers are connected. It is the healing of the masculine that needs attention here. In your cultures and in yourselves.'

Afterwards, I share the journey with the whole group. 'The Orangemen wish for healing.' I explain who they are within the politics of Northern Ireland: 'A Protestant marching organisation that keeps alive the memory of the Dutch King William of Orange. He was the one who defeated the Catholic King James at the Battle of the River Boyne in 1690.'[3]

With this clarity emerging at the end of the night, we have an acceptance that signature songs of both sides of the conflict of the North have moved into our energy field. It is a good closure of what has been a challenging day. We know now what healing we are called here to do and are ready to step up to it. Tomorrow we will design a structure to hold it.

CHAPTER THIRTEEN
A Drama at Night

Myth is a medium of magical change.
Should you choose to play a role in it,
What you do and who you are
Expands outwards.
You shape the myth and it shapes you.
Then you let it go and
It forges its own alchemy in the collective soul,
Transforming at a deep level,
What is ready to be changed.
This is the power of myth for healing.

October 1999, Glenties

On the following morning, Saturday, we tease out all of the themes coming through to us. Strengthened by the support from the spirits tangibly present in the circle now, the conflict in our group is resolved. All the themes and images from our journeys make sense:

Healing the masculine,
A new beginning,
Bear Maiden, a woman of joy,
Womb of tomorrow.
Twins in the womb,
Balance of yin and yang.
Stars healing,
Land supporting,
Rivers cleansing.

We all know the myth of Macha because we have worked with her before. Her wounding, her rage and her vulnerable time at birthing. And most of all, the reasons for putting her curse on the men of Ulster: their violation of the sacred rites of women giving birth. We ask: 'Perhaps now, in the context of all of our work over these months in Glenties, is it time to ask Macha to lift the curse off the warriors of Ulster?'

A ripple of air moves through the circle and a silence. As we begin to speak again, we are all in agreement on these themes: *Yes, the last piece of Macha's pain to be released here at Ardun. Yes, to offer a healing for the Peace Process in Northern Ireland. Yes, to have Macha galloping in on a white horse, healed and free.*

We decide to enact a mythic drama. We will do it on the hillside around the healing circle of the Celtic Mandala. For the rest of the day we make preparations to bring the Orangemen to meet Macha.

We gather this Saturday night at the field of ceremony. It is after dark and pouring rain. A fire to the side of the Celtic Mandala is blazing brightly and will be tended through the night. We make preparation to enact the drama. A chorus in the round: twelve women in all; three in each of four roles.

The Machas are standing in the West of the circle, ready to face the Orangemen who will come and stand in the East. The Crowd of Ulster is placed in the North to witness this. The Republicans, also witnesses to this encounter, are in the South with one person as Old Mother Ireland. In the realm of altered 'in-between' space, an ancient power runs through all.

As the drama begins, you can hear the three Orangemen drumming in the distance making the journey up the hill to the ceremony field. They hold themselves upright with strength and pride. They are singing a marching song, their hearts open for this meeting with Macha:

At the dark of the moon
They went to the field
To the field, to the field,
Orangemen marching, marching.
Over hill and valley,
Singing, singing.
Love in their hearts.

As those playing the role of the Orangemen arrive into the field, the drumming stops. The air is tense with expectation. The Orangemen pause before entering and move in to take up positions in the East of the circle. They look around and see the shadowed figures gathered, faces barely visible in the darkness.

Macha, the woman of the West, is waiting. She meets them with rage, these men of Ulster who caused her pain:

'I am Macha the hunted. I am Macha in pain. Do you know that, men of Ulster?'

With love in their hearts, they listen, and answer: 'We do, Macha, we do.'

All three Orangemen go to their knees and begin to speak: 'Oh, Macha, great Goddess of the West, who has been wronged by the men of Ulster, who has cursed us. We are sorry for the pain we caused you. Sorry, indeed, for our own weakness. Sorry to have violated you, stripped you of your power. We have come to ask forgiveness, come to ask you to lift your curse.'

The Orangemen stand facing her. She is dancing around, moving with such grace and authority, shifting between woman and horse. The power, vitality and sheer physical force of her is intimidating to behold. She is roaring these words at them: 'The harm caused, the years of darkness, the wars that served no-one, the hatred of each other, the lives lost in the conflict, wasted and never let go.'

Her rage is like sparks in the night air. Long hair, wild and wet. A dress of royal blue shimmering with silver. Bright colours of red ribbons streaming from her head. Pointing her finger at them. Shaking her fists and raising her head to shout at the heavens. The rain drenching her whole being. The three Orangemen say again: 'We are sorry for what we did to you, Macha, and to all women in Ulster.'

It looks like Macha has more to say to them. You can see the rage rising off her again: 'Orangemen, hear this tonight: You may say you never have taken up a gun and shot with it. But make no mistake, yours has been a powerful invisible hand behind it all. You used your power to manipulate and control every event in the province of Ulster. Out of fear, you crushed and destroyed people weaker than you. Is that not what the King of Ulster did to me? A woman about to give birth, he forced me to run the race and I fell onto the ground. In the muck of Samhain's earth I birthed my babies in front of their mocking eyes.'

A young Orangeman is thinking to himself as he listens to Macha:

I am an Ulster warrior and I do not like having to ask this. Nor having to bow my head so low to her. I am used to the power of being right. I don't want to let her have this space to rant and rave and speak against us. I want to stand up and shout NO! To argue and defend the men of Ulster. To shout her down: We will not listen any longer, woman, to your rant and rage. And yet, some force about me holds me off and says: No! You must bear the shame of what was done to her. You must hold it and not push it back. There will be no healing if you break this. So I stay in my contrite position on one knee and bowed head and, as her words flow into the night air, I let go of needing to be right. As the truth of centuries is spoken, it flows by me and is dissolving the pain. The harsh cruel hardness of the men of Ulster. Waiting and listening and swallowing all the retorts that would crush her again. And I am forced to learn in this exchange what it means to truly respect a woman and give her the space to speak her truth. I find a place in me that does not want to crush, nor destroy, nor humiliate her.

So the Orangemen all find their voices to say again to Macha: 'It was wrong what was done, we are truly sorry.' And this time it comes from a place inside them that they have never known before.

After this there is a brief pause in Macha's rant. She turns away from the Orangemen and suddenly she rises up again on her hind legs, whinnying. She turns around and, with fury, spits out her roars in the south direction where Old Mother Ireland and her sons are standing. It looks like Macha has something to say to them.

The Orangemen breathe a sigh of relief and steal a glance at each other, wondering: *Did she believe us when we said we are sorry?*

The men in the south direction of the circle begin to quiver in their boots:

We are the Republicans and we thought it would be easy this whole meeting with her. She'll be on our side. We'll be out of here and done in no time. That crowd of Orangemen will get their comeuppance from her. We'll stand here and watch all the same. Let's see them forced to bow to her. But no! Suddenly the tables have turned. Macha has changed direction and is roaring at us, asking what have we to say for the wrongs we did. The cold terror starts to run right through us. We are in such shock, shaking to the core, none of us speaks a word.

'I asked you!' Macha demands again: 'What have you to say?' Pointing at Old Mother Ireland, she roars: 'The wrongs done by your sons are not forgotten on this night either. You, too, will have to make amends before any curse is lifted here. So what have you to say?'

The Old Mother is looking at her in a shocked silence, not able to believe the words she is hearing. The terror is running right through her and all of the Republicans, stunned that Macha thinks *they* are equally at fault.

Macha berates them: 'These are not qualities that bring freedom and truth and justice to anyone. You escalated the violence and amplified the darkness behind it. Nothing excuses what you have done or how you did it. You lost sight of a noble aim. You acted with hatred and rage and a desire to maim and destroy. The damage you did brought many families to the brink and turned many towns to rubble.'

The Republicans are taken aback, uncertain as to their response:

There she is, towering above us. Shifting between woman and horse, shaking her mane. She could trample us to the ground or bolt away in her rage. We could wreck it all now if we don't say the right thing. We might not be forgiven. And everything would be lost. We are at her mercy. We thought we were less guilty and that she, the Celtic Goddess, would be on our side. We feel the shame so deeply in us, it is no longer just heavy rain that is wet on our faces but a flow of tears as we realise with full horror the part that we Republicans have played in the destruction of Ulster. We fall to our knees when the force of her words hits us. Bent to the ground underneath us, the weight of shame too heavy for our legs. Too shamed even to speak.

All of a sudden the whole place is quiet. A strange, eerie silence has descended. Everything is still except for the sound of the rain pouring down on us. We know something has changed. You can feel it in the air: Lighter ... Stronger ... Otherworldly. A sense of peace almost.

The Great Macha steps towards all of us. Her anger spent, she speaks softly and gently: 'Warriors and men of Ulster, you have heard my anger, you have listened to me. I am as tired of this curse as you are. I love the land of Ulster and I want no more bloodshed here in the name of something long gone.

'We will not bring this bitterness across the threshold of another millennium. A new time is coming and it is mine to say it: I do accept your apology. I do offer forgiveness for what was done to me and to all women and men since the birth of the Warrior era in the province of the North. We have suffered too much loss of what is precious to all of us.

'You are strong enough men. Let it go now. Rise up on your feet. Orangemen, come up off your bended knees. Republicans, let go of the shame you hold. Leave the field of battle all of you. Go home to your wives and children. Never forget what you witnessed on this hillside. You are forgiven, men of Ulster, the curse of Macha will be no more.'

She raises herself up into the stature of a Goddess. Radiant now with a strange light around her, the rain wet on her face and hair. You can hear the haunting music of the Dananns playing behind her. She speaks once more in a voice, strong and vibrant: 'Orange is the colour of my joy, green is the life force of the land.'

And with that, she walks away.

It has ceased raining and the clouds are moving rapidly across the night sky, clearing now. We look upwards and see a single star. A planet shining out in the dark of night. We have called this presence Star Bear, a fifth Goddess who brings in healing from the heavens. In an instant, the fire goes out.

Heaven's stars are sent to sing
The messages of tomorrow.
As points of dancing light above
They pierce our hearts with joy.
Will you believe what they foretell?
Forever now and always.
Crystals of wisdom shimmering there
In the bright expanse of night-time sky.

CHAPTER FOURTEEN
Macha's Joy

As joy streams through,
Synchronicities take place.
Their timing creates meaning
In a bigger story.
Pieces continue to weave
Into the fabric of the healing myth.

October 1999, Malinbeg

On the morning after the drama on the hill at Ardun, we
gather our things and pack our bags. After a last breakfast
we walk up to the field. On this Sunday morning the sun
is shining. It is the first day without rain in almost a week.
We take in the scene at the hill in daylight, remembering
what we witnessed the night before.

Standing around the circle, we thank Bear Mother and
the four Celtic Mother Goddesses for the healing given. We
bid goodbye to the spirits of the land who held this work
so safely. All twelve of us make our way back down the
hill and climb aboard the bus. Waving to Margit, we leave
Ardun House and travel up through Glengesh, along the
bouncing bog roads on the top of the mountain and down
into the valley of Glencolmcille. Within view of the sea, we
drive the last few miles to Malinbeg.

We will be here for four more days. It is *Wind Woman*, in
her mighty power, who welcomes us here: 'I am a cleansing
wind and I embrace you all. I am with you, not to batter but
to strengthen and revive you.'

Sun and wind stay with us all the next four days. It is a
time of ease and we are bursting with delight, glad to feel
the wind and sun on our faces. We twelve have great joy in
our hearts as we walk the land. We walk to the sea. Leaning
up against the cliffs, we stand chatting in the sunshine. We
drag seaweed out of the sea and drape it over our heads.
Play, beautiful play. In all of this we take time to release the
work we did at Ardun House.

In the evenings, we eat at the local restaurant and
afterwards play music and celebrate at the cottage where
we stay. At night, the stars shine in a clear sky. The moon is
waxing now to first quarter. Bathed in starlight, we search
the heavens for Star Bear's presence.

On Tuesday, we go to Slieve League, the high sea cliffs

in the southwest of Donegal. With faces raised to the mountain, we sing the story of our healing work and ask for it to be carried out across the land:

Crystal mountain, amplify our song.
Carry the blessing of this healing done,
Out to the whole of Ireland,
And allow it to support the birth of new.

As we sing, seagulls are flying, crying, above us. Bright turquoise seas swirl far beneath. Music is playing on the wind. We watch the mist clear slowly from the mountain, giving us a stark view to the top of its magnificent rugged ridges and sloping sides of scree that flow right down to the sea.

On Wednesday, we build a large mound of sand in the middle of the beach. Adorned with seaweed, shells and scattered flowers, we name it: *Breast of Woman Healing.* With drums and rattles and song, we call in the cleansing power of the sea for women's breast health everywhere and leave the mound of sand for the tide to come in, wash over the round beautiful shape of it, and take it out beyond the ninth wave.

A few days later, I am standing at the side of a lake in County Wicklow. I arrived in Glendalough the previous night, still holding a golden glow from the nine days of the Bear Medicine retreat. An autumn stillness fills the air and a soft mist hangs over the valley. I am wearing a new shawl from the woollen shop near to Malinbeg for the baptism of two baby girls. They are three-month-old twins, daughters of my dear friends from Inis Mór. One of the little girls is called Macha.

As the ceremony comes to a close, I play my fiddle to

bring in the blessing of the waters. Waves of song are faintly heard in the mist, and, from the great valley of Glendalough, I hear the spirit of the Goddess Macha speak across the waters to me: 'No greater joy at this time, after the beautiful work in Donegal, than to have twin baby girls blessed at this water's edge and one of them to carry my name.'

I rise the next morning and walk up the steep hill. I cross over a fence and see the turbulent waters of a good-sized river rising up and tumbling over large granite boulders. Torrents of white streams are moving downwards. Fresh and sparkling, tinged blue with purity.

Walking up alongside of it, I speak to the spirit of this water. Sensing a huge completion in many years of work, I ask for clarity and guidance for the next chapter of my own life. At forty-one years, I still have a deep yearning for a child of my own, brought again to my attention by the celebration of these two beautiful baby girls. *I wonder, after all of this, might I now have some babies myself? Could I step out of this work and return to an ordinary life? In a new partnership, a new beginning, in a new millennium?*

I see the colours of the water swirling back and forth as they gush downwards. Their pale blue and turquoise pulls me in. I am taken back in time to a druidic era in Ireland when things of old were breaking down and an arrogance came to people who were spiritual then. I see a thousand worlds within this one, all interlaced, sparkling and changing. A spirit voice answers me:

An instant in time will change your fate forever.
The feminine was being ignored in this era.
Women priestesses were being crushed, abused and ridiculed,
Forced out of their places.
Spiritual power taken from them. Stripped.
Men rising to dominate.

A deep quiet comes into me and I see a picture of the Grandmothers of 'past, present and future' who have been guiding this journey all along. I sense their comforting presence around me within these waters and their messages in my head. Ancient women, they are yearning for women's truth to be seen again in the rivers, the forests, and the mountains:

Seek it not, Daughter,
Your fate is sealed
With the ancient spirit of this land.
The rivers will run free again.
The women will come forth
Carrying torches of light
That will spread out across the land,
Clearing it of all the past.
You can choose, of course,
But choose wisely, in line with the stars.

As I listen, I see a picture of women everywhere singing from the hilltops. A gentle light emanating. The wise women restored to guide and help. The rivers are clean to wash the new-born. The image fades and I blink myself back into this reality, filling my lungs with the early morning Wicklow air. Releasing myself and renewing the decision to serve. A prickling of tears. The babies are not to be – at least not for now. I let it go completely.

~

I go back to Malinbeg to clear the cottage of all of our things. I walk the beach at Silver Strand with a man I love. I met him three years ago when I first moved to Donegal.

He is a man of the sea. I call him a prince of the Dananns. A son of Manannán mac Lir.[1] He has that kind of light.

He knows all of the stars and constellations in the sky – Orion, Cassiopeia, Castor and Great Bear. He can point a finger at every planet as it moves through the heavens. The twinkling blue of Venus, distant red of Mars and the shining white of Jupiter.

Over the years that I have known him, this captain of the stars, I have woven the patterns of our love into the seas and mountains, rivers and lakes of Donegal. Allowing my joy to sing out, I gave thanks for the light that's given in sweet times of ease.

Today is a beautiful day here in Malinbeg. Gracious, gentle sunshine lights up the land, showing us the colours and shapes of the rocks. The whole place is an amazing array of peace and beauty.

This day, walking the beach, we are looking at the high-tide mark. A full moon is coming up in a few days and we are observing just how high up the waxing moon tides come on the west coast of Ireland in the autumn.

This one has brought in a gift of hundreds of oranges. 'Don't kick the orange,' he says to me, teasing of my shamanic work, 'you'll hurt its feelings.' I look again and realise there are hundreds of oranges spread in an arc along the high-water mark across the whole length of beach. And suddenly it clicks with me: 'Of course ... oranges ... the Orangemen!'

A box of them must have been dumped at sea – but I prefer the mythic message that is speaking in this. A gift from the folk who live out beyond the ninth wave, acknowledging the work done. Often, when it speaks within a myth, the universe has a very artistic touch and a great sense of humour. I bend down to pick up an orange. And I turn to whisper into the wind: 'Orange is the colour of your joy, Macha, and today it is mine also.'

My companion, the Star Captain, has walked back along to the rocks. I turn away from the sea and walk back to join him. His handsome profile is etched against the cliffs. I look upwards to see a single seagull flying over, calling its cry above us. He is fascinated with the geology of this place. 'This must be shale ... it's easy to crumble. I suppose these stones have feelings, too?' He asks so humorously that I burst out laughing. Mischievously, he smiles, nudges me up against a large stone and folds me into his arms in a soft and gentle embrace. He says: 'This rock will have a new story to tell, the next time you speak to it.'

CHAPTER FIFTEEN
Samhain Bear

Standing at the threshold
Of Bear's winter dreaming time,
Pointing the way to the cave.
What do you release?
What seeds of the new
Do you take into the womb
Of winter's dark?
Such is Samhain Bear,
Asking us to know.
Know ourselves.

November 1999, Glenties

On the second weekend in November, four of us gather again at Ardun House. It is over a month since the Bear Medicine retreat and we are into a new moon cycle. We have come this weekend to do a shamanic workshop called *Samhain Bear*. Samhain is the time of descent into the womb of winter in the Celtic calendar, and in the practice of Bear Medicine we also honour this time for the hibernation of Mother Bear. This is the time of year when we fatten our souls to sustain our light in the months of winter.

We gather at dusk on Friday evening and step outside to drum and sing with the waxing crescent moon. In our circle the following morning we are shown, through journeys, what to do: we four have been called here to clear the land and to close down the energy of all of the work. We are to take time to thank the spirits of the land for what has been held here through the years of transformation in all of these gatherings with Bear Mother, Macha and the other Celtic Goddesses.

We four women are clear and wise in our knowing. We come with the ability and practised skill to hold the level of work that will release the land from being a vessel and send the helping spirits into a winter sleep.

In the afternoon we go out on our separate ways to give thanks. We bury our faces into the green of the earth and breathe into it, the energy of release. I am shown to go up the hill and dance the whole story: from the very beginning to the very end. Every stage and each group that continued it – since the first glimpse of Macha and the Ulstermen at the dinner table in the Highlands Hotel, right through to the lifting of the curse last month. In pale November sunshine I find a flat green space up high, overlooking the whole valley, and I dance it all.

On Sunday morning we gather outside, just before dawn,

to watch the sunrise coming forth after the ceremony for
hibernation that we did the night before.

Sister sun, sister sun,
You are in the sky
Red and beautiful.
We see your tracks in the sky
Spread out from behind the mountain peaks,
Although you have not yet risen.
Thank you for the gift of dawn.
A dance of harmony.
Sun and moon.
Male and female.
Light and dark.
Know the depth of this teaching:
'Everything that is normally dominant
Has to learn a new dance.'

In this brightness of autumn today, and Bear Mother
going to rest, we believe the land is closing down just for
this winter. Come the spring, surely we will gather again
here for new work? Today, we do not know that there never
will be another gathering of women outside on the hill at
Ardun House in Glenties.

Margit will close down the healing centre and sell her
house. She will build a new home further up the hill on her
land. What is remembered and what has been given to us
by the spirits of the land at Ardun will be carried forth. It
will always be there ...

That hillside with the fire in the centre surrounded by a
Mandala of four colourful prayer sticks for Macha, Brigid,
Danu and Morrígan. There is a circle of women standing
around it with faces raised to the sun. Full of warmth and
the beauty of sisterhood, a blessing of sparkling magic is
tangible in their midst.

EPILOGUE
A New Millennium

Brigid, you are guide of the women,
Oh, Brigid, you are shaman of the soul.
What is it you would have us do?
What is it you would have us do?

When you light the fires in Belfast,
You call the soul back home.

December 1999, Donegal

The months after the drama with Macha in Glenties are the most blessed with miracles that I have seen in a long time. As the millennium draws to a close, after many years of intense healing work, I have a sense of transcendence and great joy. It vibrates in every cell of my body. You cannot explain what has happened, but you know that the work has reached a place of profound healing in the collective soul of women.

You know it makes a difference. The women and the Great Celtic Mothers have birthed it together – a new energy for the future.

This is the power that women have. It does not belong to us, it is a gift of light given, flowing through. There is a choice: Do we use this power to bless or to curse? When we ask to receive it, and work towards the highest good, this light shows itself in a myriad of ways that connect with the intelligence of a bigger story. You learn to read the signs and follow their lead. You hold the tension of aeons of women's suffering. And yet you can hold it, for you are helped by forces from beyond to do this.

I am eternally grateful to all of the women of courage who walked with me on this journey to meet Macha in her wounded self in the wild landscapes of Inis Mór and west Donegal.

January 2000, Belfast

The new millennium of 2000 dawned six weeks after we closed down our work at Glenties with *Samhain Bear*. At the end of January, I went to Belfast as an invited facilitator with the organisation called Feminism and Religion to join in their annual Imbolc celebration of Brigid as Celtic Mother Goddess and Saint.[1]

In the latter months of 1999, the Northern Ireland Peace Process had resulted in the first new power-sharing government since 1974. At the turn of the millennium it was in its fragile beginnings. It crashed miserably in the middle of January 2000.

All of this was still in the air in the North as 120 women from all over Ireland gathered in Stranmillis College in Belfast to celebrate Imbolc in a workshop called: *Brigid: Soulsmith for a New Millennium.* A very fitting title coined by the organising group.

The weekend included workshops, crafting, musical performances, ceremony, and the lighting of the Brigid's Fires. The theme of the weekend honoured the mythology of Brigid as Goddess of fire and patron of the blacksmith's forge.

When we light the fires in Belfast,
We call the soul back home.[2]

BOOK TWO

Healing Light in Ulster

PART I

The Soul of Ulster

CHAPTER ONE
A Fairy Glen

Our land is marked out
With ancient pathways of power,
Laid down before the time of
The Tuatha Dé Danann.
The megalithic stone sites
Connect the energy of the land
With the movement of the stars.
Known to holy women and ancient druids,
And carried through the centuries by the fairy folklore,
The practices of natural wisdom arising from these alignments
Were used to support healing, divination, fertility
And the health and prosperity of the land.

2000-2011, Donegal

In the years after 2000, the nature of the healing work I was doing changed. I sensed a new light coming in. It was a golden light that infused everything and after so many years of transforming the shadows, it was very welcome. A time of great ease that brought a subtle shimmering of new things, flowing in like a river. During all of these 'golden years', I didn't hear much from Macha. Everything had settled into a vibration of peace.

I had negotiated the purchase of a beautiful two-acre site in a glen at Tirrion in Inishowen in the most northerly part of Donegal, one of the nine historic counties of Ulster. Subject to planning permission, the site was southeast facing and bordered top and bottom with rows of sycamore trees. It stretched right down to the river in the valley.

Cold in winter, but sheltered from the prevailing westerly winds, it is land that is richly wooded and stays green throughout the year. The Long Glen river flows through the valley here and reaches the sea, half a mile northwards, at Kinnego Bay.

At the winter solstice in December 2008, my friend Peter and I plotted the fence posts for the site and the outline of the house. I remember that day clearly. We worked all day in heavy rain and wind but the strong energy supported us to finish it within the short hours of daylight.

Through the winter of 2009 I collaborated with a talented architect to design my home. He had an instinct to preserve what was already there and an eye for a design that reflected the natural line of the land. I measured every window and door and ensured it was just the right size to frame a view of the sea or to catch the sight of a special tree in the distance. The house was to be a structure of beauty, with its curved walls, small windows at the back, and large windows and a sunroom at the front. By the summer of

2010 we had obtained full planning permission to build.

At the same time, I hired some very skilled and wonderful men to renovate a small cottage on the laneway of Tirrion and I secured a lease on this for five years. With a new oak floor, and light coming in from the south, this little house was to be a bright and cosy sanctuary for work and writing until my own home was built.

September 2011, Donegal

It is almost twelve years since the autumn of 1999 in Glenties when we did the healing work with Macha. I am standing on a hill in Tirrion, looking down on another green valley. There is a special glow of magic in this glen. I cannot describe the feeling in words that I have whilst being here. It is a deep-grounded soulfulness, serene and calm. Not wild or elemental, but a safe sanctuary that, like a beloved, wraps me in a blanket of peace and belonging. Every tree, every stone and each river welcomes me and speaks to me. Never alone, I am giving and receiving every time I walk here.

I often spend a few hours walking in the valley. I have several places where I stop and sit. A tree I call 'Sycamore Mother' is part of a row of trees just up from the river. I can lie in a hollow at her base and take in the afternoon sunshine. At the waterfall, I lie on a mossy bank listening to the sound of the water and sensing the presence of fairy folk. At the stone wall that slopes down the field, I sit and play my drum. The sea air blows in on this boundary wall and daffodils bloom here in the springtime. In the woods close to the old houses, I can rest on the grass and look up through the new soft green leaves of the trees and see the sky.

In my eye line, the trees of Tirrion are special. Some were placed and tended by the ancestors over generations and they blend in now with autumn colours. Others grow wild on the hillsides like the rowans visible everywhere with their red swathes of berries marking out their places on the land. A big holly in the valley is guardian to all. Beside the river is a hawthorn, sprinkling its red berries onto the grass underneath. I bend to pick up a piece of branch covered in green furry lichen. Such blessings to be here, magical and pure. The deepest sense of home I have ever known.

It is like the places where my mother's kinfolk were reared. I remember childhood summers spent in Torr and Murlough, the wild headlands and rocky bays that mark out the north Antrim coast from Ballycastle to Cushendun. With the smell of honeysuckle in the summer and the sight of red fuchsia hedges along all the roads, those places, too, carry the magic of fairy folk. The old houses here at Tirrion put me in mind of my Granda James' family homestead at Torr. It must be these memories in my bones that make this place feel so much like home.

Just over a month ago, after about six years of not hearing much from her, Macha came back into my life. In July 2011, on a visit to Emain Macha in County Armagh, and in conversation with two of the staff at the interpretative centre, we discovered a shared passion for Macha's place in the mythic history of Ulster. It was then that I received the invitation to give a talk about my work with Macha over the years.

This recent contact with Macha is the beginning of a new journey with her. This time, we will cross 'the border', and the journey will continue, she tells me, within the six counties of the North.

A car pulls up at the little house in Tirrion. Four of us get out and stretch. My brother James with his wife, Maggy, and daughter Hannah have come to stay with me in Moville for a few days. They all enjoy this area around Kinnego Bay and they take in deep breaths of the sea air as they look around. We change our shoes for a long hike into the valley and up over the hills, excited to be out here for a day's walk.

Hannah had a twin sister, Jeanette, who died when eight months old on the winter solstice of 1991. Like a little white dove of peace, her spirit is still with them. Here, in the magic of Tirrion, is a place to be with that little girl-soul who resides in the world of the fairy people.

Having gathered our things and put our lunch in the house for later, we head off down the lane and across the field and along the line of trees at the top end of the site. After we have taken some time to look at the views, we continue down the slope to the fuchsia hedge. Bending our heads, we move through the thick tunnel of branches and come out at the lower, most magical, part of the site.

We can see the river in the valley and we make our way down and across it, balancing our steps on the stones in the middle. Trekking across the flat, open field and heading for the forest, we are like four hobbits pushing our way into the Elven domain of Rivendell. Keeping the forest and the waterfall beneath us on the right, we follow the path up beyond the tree line and step out onto boggy terrain. We jump from clump to clump of rushes and pick our steps through the longer grass, until we emerge out onto the scrubland of heather and small bushes at Doult Bridge, where the turf road leads up to the bog.

From here we can see the whole valley stretched out in front of us. Houses are dotted across the hills and we see the blue of the sea beyond. The line of the boundary fence for my site is clearly visible and I love to see its place within all of the large green fields within the whole beautiful neighbourhood of this glen. We take pictures of the little house, looking bright on this glorious day.

From Doult Bridge we hike over the bog road and this takes us down to the main glen road. From there, we go along the last half mile back to the little house. With the bright sun streaming in the window, and tucking into a lovely lunch, this is a day to remember. Although I do not realise it today, this walk will prove to be very significant in the years to come.

CHAPTER TWO
A Shadow Passes Over

Shine out your light
With the poetry of Ireland.
Shine out your light
In the stillness of the dawn.
Shine out your light
In the embrace of the mountains.
Call the Ulster soul home.
This is the place that
Held all the shadow,
Held all the darkness,
Held all the pain.
This is the place
That's been crushed
And downtrodden.
Call the Ulster soul home.

March 2012, Tirrion

It is a month now since my talk in Armagh. The recent promptings from Macha and the reaction of the audience convince me that she is asking that I write a new narrative that will record her role in the healing of the land and soul of Ulster. Having lifted the curse, Macha is determined to play her part in bringing harmony and reconciliation to the people of Ulster.

Within the mild days of March, I walk the beach in the mornings and do my T'ai Chi. As I gather the threads for this writing, I glimpse stories shimmering in the sea. I begin to notice things around me. I listen to Macha's voice as she guides the flow of the writing.

I reflect on the past winter of 2011. Those months that followed the lovely walk with my brother and his family in September. That day marked out the last time that I was out on the land without a sense of disturbance. Since then, something is wrong here at Tirrion. Too many things have happened that have shaken the quiet peace of this valley. I have watched and noticed a disturbance of the harmony that drew me here. Animals are hunted in the night-time, their dens dug out and left as piles of soil on the tender green of the land. The savage tear of a digger snarling back and forth as trees are torn asunder in the valley. A notice for windmills went up in January. The early signs of the despoliation of the land that is to come.

Over that winter, I was drawn deeper into the shadow of what had gone before. The land was, and still is, speaking of sorrow, ancient and deep. Rituals at the rivers, songs in the mountain and conversations with the trees revealed to me what lies in the emotional memory of the whole glen. I am seeing images from the past. Famine, landlords and Church oppression. Places where the people could not take full possession of their own land, and as they remained servile to an unseen force, the land absorbed their unspoken fear, pain and shame.

One day, Macha lands into my room in the little house. The place fills with warmth and a faint fragrance of summer flowers. Dressed in a gown of red and grey, she stands at the window, looking out. Deep in thought, she is quiet and I stay in the silence with her. Eventually she is ready to talk. I tell her of the streams of images and signs that I saw over the winter. I ask her: 'What is the meaning of these?'

Macha turns round, answering my question: 'The presence of the fox protects the wild spirit of any land and when the badger is hunted, the boundaries of the land are not protected.'

As she continues, she has turned away again and is staring out of the window in a trance. Filled with the power of generations of memory, she continues: 'There are patterns of soul loss and abuse all over the land in Ireland, held in the memory of the water and the stones. This is what happens to the earth's life force when there is trauma, war or misuse of the land. The spirit departs and the land becomes empty and dead.'[1]

'Hitherto, the fairy paths and solitary hawthorns protected the soul of the land and were left alone. This was respected as the lore of the fairy folk, who are the descendants of the Tuatha Dé Danann within the land. Handed down through the stories of the Sídhe, these traditions are still alive today in rural Ireland. Farmers throughout the country were connected to this natural wisdom. They paid attention to the cycles of the moon and the changes in the air at each season. They knew the cure for many ailments.

'Maintaining a rhythm of ritual throughout the year, ordinary folk were assured of protection, health and wellbeing, year in, year out, as the cosmic wheel turned, no matter what challenges they faced.'[2]

I sense a pause. A presence is coming into the room.

A woman's spirit. I know this one. She is a Grandmother of this land, whose kind presence I have felt here before, welcoming me, glad someone will be living again on her land. She reared a family in this glen in the early 1900s. Macha stops, smiles and invites her to sit and says: 'You have heard what we are talking about and you are coming in to join us?'

'Yes,' the Grandmother says and smiles. 'I am glad to be here with you.' Her dark hair is wrapped in a bun and a rough cotton ribbon is tied around it. She is wearing an apron of bright colours with a thick red skirt underneath. The sleeves of an old beige gansey are visible and her hands, lying folded in her lap, are strong and sunburned.

'There is so much we didn't know in our day and it is good to sense the fairy folk coming alive again. But the shadows ...' she shakes her head and sighs. 'The shadows were always on the edges, too. We didn't pay any attention to them.'

Macha nods at her, inviting her to continue, and her story unfolds:

'We were happy in this glen. We loved the land and we worked on it all the hours that God sent. We had a good herd of sheep on the hill, and a few pigs we would rear and sell. We had enough to eat with milk and butter from the cows and eggs from the hens. We planted vegetables out in front. If we were lucky we had the salted herring for the winter months. And we'd knit ganseys and socks from the wool we'd spun. We'd make our clothes from odd pieces of cloth we could buy. All the women worked the farms as well as the men. And the whole family worked the land. Winter and summer.[3]

'Nicholson was the landlord here in this glen, and he would visit his house for the summer. He was a decent man, and for the most part left us in peace. He gave plenty of work to the men around, planting and weeding the turnips or cutting his turf. The women worked inside the big house and served in the dining room. He donated land for a school to be built for the children.[4]

'We were, of course, beholden to him. 'Twas his place, he owned all the farms around here in the glen. When he passed by on his horse, we would stop our work and nod our respects to him. We may not have owned this land but we were happy nonetheless.[5] We were left in peace to live off it and rear our children as best we could.

'And as you say, we knew about the fairies and their paths through the land. We were kept safe by them as long as we left them alone. We didn't say too much about the fairies to the priest of the parish.'

When the Grandmother stops speaking, I sense the fairy folk gathering at the door to listen to her. Macha is smiling.

'Yes,' says Macha, 'the early Celtic Christian Church in Ireland respected this lore as part of the natural spirituality. The land was feminine and wild and allowed to remain as such. It was revered. The early Roman Church preyed upon these cosmic blessings and made taboo the belief in the fairy folk. They pulled us into a doctrine of obedience and took what they wanted of our places of spirit, changing their natural cosmic signatures to fit their own new code.'[6]

Macha asks me: 'Does any of this help you to understand what is going on here?'

I am nodding my head and have a great sense of peace since the Grandmother has come in to speak with us. I say: 'Yes, as I listen to all of this, I can see that within the memory of the stones and the waters of the land of Ireland, the patterns that the Church laid down are as hard to heal as the patterns of servitude, embedded here during the era of the landlords.'

Macha continues: 'While the English colonised our land and minds, the Churches imprisoned our souls and colonised the core of our being. The seedbed where the new is generated. Imprinting everything born with the unredeemable sin of Eve. This they did over the whole land. All of it still holds generations of sadness and loss.'

We three sit in the silence. There is plenty more that could be said about the isolation felt in Donegal after partition came about in 1922. What was originally the nine-county mythical province of Ulster became the six-county province of Northern Ireland.[7] The grief and rage felt by many people in the six counties that were annexed from the rest of Ireland are still festering in the collective psyche of the North. The separation and grief experienced by the land and people of Donegal, Cavan and Monaghan in the partition of historic Ulster have never much been acknowledged or spoken about.

It seems, however, that we have talked enough for today. The Tirrion Grandmother is smiling her goodbyes and leaves with the song of fairy folk echoing behind her. Macha stands up, also ready to depart, and says: 'It is healing enough sometimes to just talk.'

Spring 2012

There is a small, dead white horse in the field next to here. The carcass lies on the other side of the boundary wall. I saw it first about six weeks ago in January when I was preparing the talk on Macha and I wondered then what was its significance. After I saw it, I got word to the horse dealer who owned it. He appeared on my doorstep the following Sunday and said he would have to bury it. A few weeks later, as I took a walk down the hill, the smell at the top of the field told me the dead horse was still lying there, undisturbed and starting to rot.

Today, I choose to walk on the other side of the land to avoid the horse. I climb over the gate and walk across the roadway and down towards the trees at the seaward side of the land. This brings me to the stone wall on the site where I will build my house. A special rowan is beside the wall, and a hawthorn and a spreading old holly tree bend themselves over the wall on this side of the land. And here I am, sitting on the grass by the new yellow daffodils. The air brings a light breeze across the land and I can smell the sea. I drum gently, connecting with the spring sunshine and the newly awakened earth. Macha comes to sit beside me. I ask her: 'Where should I start writing today?'

She says, 'Write about the dead horse. A dead horse on the land is not a good sign.'

I sigh and know that this does not bode well. Although it is across the wall in the neighbour's land, it is affecting the whole valley in its decaying, awful, neglected state. I pack my drum in its bag and walk back up the field, picking my way along the boundary fence.

At the top, in an adjacent field, I see a large white cow just over the fence of the neighbouring farm. She is sheltering in the shade of the trees and is turned away from me. As I look closely, I see long strands of glistening red innards stringing out of her backside. I realise with a start that she has just given birth.

I look closer and see a little white calf huddled on the ground beside her, hidden by the shade and the long grass. Its fur is still wet from the animal womb waters. Smiling, I lean over the fence and say to the mother cow: 'I will not harm you or your calf. Do not be afraid.' I lie down on the grass and bury my face into the fresh green growth. I am so grateful to be in the presence of birth. Birth, birth, fresh, green, wonderful birth.

I walk back to the cottage and sit at my desk facing the sun. On finishing my writing about the dead horse, I watch two hawks flying in slow circles in the sky beyond my window. Not coming often, it is a special treat to see them. My spirit soars with them, uplifting everything. I believe they show themselves high in the sky when energy has been released and their presence here today tells me that these cycles of 'death' and 'birth' that I have witnessed all winter have been registered energetically in the invisible world of this valley.

Light comes to renew and reclaim us back from the darkness. From September to Samhain to winter solstice, to Imbolc and now at spring equinox. All through a winter of endless rain and dark days, I have watched and waited.

Light comes in to release the old. Spring awakens and winter recedes. Rays of the sun are streaming out of the clouds, lighting up the whole hillside. I am knowing that it is now time for the land to be free again.

To have a home built on a site with fresh green earth and a healed feminine spirit within the land of Ireland – that is my deepest desire and has remained so for many years. But I have found this winter harsh on my soul and spirit. There have been so many signs that seem to contradict my choice to settle in Tirrion. At this point, I do not know what has happened to the original 'call' to come here and build.

At Eastertime I call on three friends, Celia, Liam and Tom, who practise shamanism, to join me on the land and help find out from the spirits here if I should proceed with the plan to build.

In the dreamtime place of drum and song, we see the spirits of four horses gather at the top of the road into the glen: 'We will come no further,' they say, 'in respect for the spirit of the dead horse which has long since risen out beyond this valley of tears.'

All of our journeys to the helping spirits concur: 'This is not a place for her to settle in. It would take a lot of effort to make it work, and difficult to maintain the energetic boundaries on this land in the years to come. The little house will remain protected for a few more years so it is safe to hold for now.'

One of my companions sees in the world of 'spirit essence' a deer calf in the corner of a field, newly born and fragile. He hears these words spoken for me: 'This baby deer spirit is yours, the fruit of your work, but it does not belong here on this land and will not thrive.'

The gentle presence of spirit Grandmothers enters the room to hold and nurture all of what has been shown to us. They say: 'The new light on this land will be held now. This glen is your home and you will always belong here, but you will have another place to put down your roots.'

One Sunday in early May, I spend a whole day in communion with the Spirit of the Wind. A wonderful morning of meditation and prayer. Outdoors all afternoon. So rich, so deep, to see the power of this wind. Cleansing, sweeping, lifting, releasing, everything in the land. Across the grass. In the flowers. Through the trees in the valley. Holly shimmering. Slender, young rowans bending over. Sycamores rustling with orchestral power. Birds carried on airstreams soaring about the sky. Magnificent wind. Powerful, benevolent, cleansing spirit. A life force so pure.

Watching this energy sweep through the whole valley, all in its path is washed clean with this force today. A fresh new day. Exhilaration. I run up and down the fields with arms outstretched enjoying the uplift. I take my fiddle outside to play. Heart and magic. Giving thanks. Free.

Later in the month of May, I watch and wait and finally see the land return to light. At the new moon just past Bealtaine, you can sense the spirit of renewal. In the early morning stillness, fairy singing can be heard. In Danu's warm embrace, the earth is blossoming. Great peace fills the air. Birds are singing. I watch the green grass shimmering as I sit underneath the sycamore trees near the old homesteads. Primroses are sprouting up within a circle of yellow daffodils. And, looking down the hill, I feel a great warmth. A fresh new vitality has entered here, bringing the ancestors out to dance in the lanes. Celebrating, and with a gentle softness of being, they all give their thanks. The Grandmother speaks to me. She thanks me for the tension I have held through a winter of endless rain and dark days: 'God bless you!' she says, 'healing has come to the land.'

CHAPTER THREE
Memories

There is a still point in the centre.
A small, still voice of peace
Is holding the way forward.
A door opens and you go through.
There is light and warmth beyond.
The history is clearing now.
Choices are there to create a new land,
Creating new memories and new life.

May 2012, Tirrion

Through these months, as spring moves into summer, the elements have brought a great healing and release in the land. The presence of my own Grandmother, Katie, is very strong these past few weeks here at Tirrion. She was my father's mother and died in 1949, nine years before I was born. My Grandmother was a teacher and her spirit is with me today as I am writing. I look out the window and sense my girl-soul dancing in the field beyond. The little girl who loves this fairy place. I sense Grandmother Katie's spirit at the side of the field, watching:

> *There is a little girl,*
> *She is in a green field,*
> *She is dancing.*
> *Take her hand.*
> *Watch her body move*
> *In time with the flow.*
> *Watch her feet on the earth*
> *And the joy in her face.*
> *... la la la le la ... la la la le la ...*
> *You see a little girl*
> *Sitting by a stream.*
> *She is singing,*
> *Listening to the music of the waters.*
> *Watch the words*
> *Moving on her lips.*
> *Watch the light*
> *On her face*
> *And see that she is at home.*
> *There is a robin*
> *Singing its song*
> *On the hedge,*
> *Branches bare since winter.*

The little girl watches from the window.
She sees gorse on the hedges
Beyond the field,
Bright and yellow.
Here is a little girl
Who is welcoming spring.
This little girl is
Cuddled in a chair
By the fire.
Take her in your arms
Take her home.

By early June it is becoming clear to me that the rocks, trees, stones and rivers, along with the elements and the sheer beauty of this glen, have, together, become an alchemical vessel to hold a wider healing of the soul of Ulster.

The sea, as I look out at it this morning, is playing its part in the offering of light, the blue of its holding, the high vibration of its silver water, the wildness of its dance. There is a fierce power of transformation in the rolling waves.

I am sitting with Macha at my little house in the glen. She is dressed in a gown of lavender and pink, flecked with silver. When the sun catches her dark hair you can see the threads of grey in it. We are talking about trauma and soul loss within the North of Ireland.

I can see that Macha, in the weaving of this new narrative, is calling home all the lost soul parts of this land here in Donegal and in the six counties of the North. I breathe deeply as she shows me the pictures of the town in County Antrim where I grew up in the 1960s.

'There are many towns in the North that need healing,' Macha tells me. 'This is a journey to bring the heart home, to bring back the kindness lost to everyone in the shadows of war. For you, Daughter, concern yourself only with this.'

My Grandmother Katie's spirit reaches across the veils

of time and comes into the room to speak to us about her life in Lisburn in the 1920s. As she sits with us, I see her round plump face is kindly and strong. She is wearing a cardigan of pale beige and a skirt of plaid, a mix of creams and browns. Her hair is drawn back in a bun. Her eyes look sad to me, and I see a lifetime of memories fleeting across her face. But she is enveloped in an air of warmth and kindness that never left her in spite of the years of darkness.

She speaks gently: 'We stood there in the front garden and watched a mob of looters drag all our furniture and belongings out of the house, pile it up and dowse it with petrol. A match was struck and it all went up in flames. Everything we had was burnt.'

Macha comments: 'Like so many other mothers all across Ulster, the heart of her family was destroyed by war and troubles.'

I spend three days sitting with Macha, witnessing these past events and talking to my Grandmother. It is as though I am looking at a film screen on the wall that shows me pictures of the burnings in Lisburn in August and September 1920. Shops, pubs and homes were set on fire in many of the streets of the town and were left burning for days in smouldering pyres of sectarian hatred. The air is dark and heavy with dust. I can smell the charred remains and see the terror on stricken faces. The whole place is reverberating with shock.[1]

I see a vision of my Grandmother as she kneels praying in the church a day or two afterwards. Her head is bent and her eyes are brimming with tears, but she is too proud to give into those. She is asking for the strength to keep going. Asking for simple things; boxes to sit on, a table to eat at. And help and protection for her family. I hear her silent petition: *How can we continue when all of my own are leaving the town?*

When the pictures finally fade from the screen on the wall with us, Macha says: 'The heart of that town was destroyed for everyone, as were many others at the time. We will call in the power of the Rose Quartz crystal to bring harmony and to help clear these memories of the past. We will connect this light with all of those shamanic gatherings in Arizona, on Cruit Island, and in Hope Springs in Ohio, when a Rose Quartz crystal was used for healing in the North of Ireland.

'Do you remember the man from Donaghadee at your talk in February at Emain Macha? He asked about the big Rose Quartz crystal. Glowing all evening, the crystal brought harmony. You also took that Rose Quartz into the valley last winter to offer healing when the trees were cut down. The power of it is already vibrating in this land. It is the healing of the heart we want now.'

I deepen my breath and move into that 'in-between-altered-place', sitting again in silence beside Macha and my Grandmother, and looking at the film screen on the wall.

As I look more closely, I see soft rays of rose-pink light come in and flow like a river through all of the streets of Lisburn town. The ethereal light streams around every burning remains. It envelops the people who were huddled in corners weeping with shock and loss, their faces smudged with soot and tears. It continues flowing past them and on up the street, and through smouldering buildings, around lanes and cul-de-sacs of houses, and finally moving off along the River Lagan flowing towards the sea. I watch the light from the Rose Quartz transforming and softening, releasing and dissolving, the memories still held in the invisible corners of this town.

As the images fade and we gradually come out of the vision of it all, Macha turns to me and says kindly: 'You took in too much of the shadow of that town as an infant in the hospital when you were fighting for your life for weeks on end. You've carried this story far too long. I think this might be the end of it.'

Deep in her thoughts, my Grandmother nods. In this moment, watching her, I know she has been walking with me all my life, protecting me. I was named for her, and her eyes, as she turns to look at me, are shining with love.

By the end of the conversation, my Grandmother has left us and is walking outside on the lane looking over the fuchsia hedges and smiling. She looks happy now, lighter somehow, and is speaking in low tones. Perhaps giving thanks for everything that we have shared these past days. Perhaps to her husband, John, and her children. Perhaps to the ancestors here at Tirrion. I hear her voice coming through to us in the house, a gentle singing voice that never left her:

> *And tones that are tender and tones that are gruff*
> *Are whispering over the sea ...*
> *Come back, Paddy Reilly, to Ballyjamesduff*
> *Come home, Paddy Reilly, to me.*[2]

PART II

Mending the Heart

CHAPTER FOUR
Rose Quartz

A Rose Quartz crystal
Walked its way to the forgotten counties of Ireland,
Those six they called the North
When they separated that land
From the mother source in the South.
Rose Quartz carries the song lines
From Oracle to Ulster.
I hear songs in the air as I return,
Bringing back the sweetness
To the streets and the park.

June 2012, Donegal

After the summer solstice, I sense a shift. The energy from the Rose Quartz healing with Macha and Grandmother Katie in Tirrion has taken root. When I look back over the years, I can see a tapestry of events that formed a backdrop to that healing.

In the first spring of the new millennium, April 2000, I went to an International Shamanic gathering in Oracle, Arizona. It was organised by Tending Sacred Circles, a group of dedicated practitioners from different countries. I joined with my Bear Sister colleagues and Carol Proudfoot-Edgar, my Bear Medicine teacher, along with 130 other people to create ceremonies in the desert for healing in the world.[1]

It took several months to prepare the creative form we brought to Oracle. Lines woven in the dreamtime through the hibernation of winter. We crafted a beautifully sculpted world in many colours in the desert sand. Each country was painted in. Mountains were built in the sand, some with snow on top. Rivers of blue flowed across continents. Each country was aligned with crystals set at the North Pole, connected to the core of the earth and reaching upwards to the stars.

The crystals carried the healing from the centre of this world map to the many lands across the world. Crystals pulsating with the deep knowing. Mother Earth is calling us home. It was Jo, Bear Sister from Tucson, who placed the Rose Quartz on the North of Ireland.

We sang our healing intentions at Oracle and sent them out across the world. We knew, even as our 'world sculpture' was being dismantled and returned to the desert sand, that the mending would continue long afterwards.

The song lines we had created would carry the power of these crystals into the dreamtime. Following these invisible energy lines across the world, the crystals would continue their healing for many years after.

When I returned to Ireland I began to reflect on all of this work. I considered: *How does this healing energy manifest?* I started working with crystals in Arizona and a different world of healing opened to me after that gathering in Oracle.

From there on, I did even more subtle energy work, learning more about crystals and the sending of healing intentions along the song lines, those invisible lines of energy that carry the songs of the crystals across the world for the highest good. I learned how to keep positive thoughts moving in a stream towards consciousness. I navigated the shadows that would inevitably come to challenge the flowing in of a higher vibration of light.

The job of energy workers is simply to trust what is called and trust in the unfolding of events around us. The direction of the healing is orchestrated by intelligence beyond us. We continue to do our work for the highest good, and we trust that when the time is right, we may be called in, as agents, to assist a wider healing. The energy for such healing has been collectively built and nurtured by a large number of people over many years, manifesting itself here in our world by beings of light from the unseen worlds.

Sometimes you can see with great clarity how the energy is weaving in these worlds beyond us. We may be shown a whole pattern of what is being healed, how it is being healed, and how the energy of light is moving through the systems around us. It is the power of clear intention that can imbue a crystal with a healing energy.

Another pivotal experience on the journey with Rose Quartz healing came in July 2007. I was invited to join in a crystal healing ceremony for *Light in Ireland* organised by a team from the Vibrational Healing Foundation, based in London. At that time they were doing ground-breaking work in Derry, training people in crystal and spiritual healing.[2]

On that extraordinary day in Derry, with over forty people present, the power of twenty-two large Rose Quartz crystals was linked into one intention and attuned for healing in Ireland. I was asked to play music during the ceremony. I met a number of skilled crystal healers and energy workers and enjoyed the connection with them. A new pathway was opening that would move us all in the years to come towards peace and healing in the North of Ireland.

At the end of that day, one of the twenty-two large Rose Quartz crystals was given to me to support my work in Donegal and the North. It was a great privilege to receive this gift and it sits on a stand of oak in my front room in Moville. In the five years since, it has travelled with me to various places in Ireland. It is this beautiful crystal that I took to the evening presentation at Emain Macha in February 2012.

A few days after the summer solstice, at the end of June 2012, I am sitting at my kitchen table in my house in Moville. I am aware of my Grandmother's presence around me. It seems she has more to say about the 1920s. She takes a seat in the armchair by the open door and looks out at my garden.

In 1920, my Grandmother Katie lived on the Antrim Road in Lisburn. She had six children, the eldest was fifteen and my father, Michael, who was eight years old at the time, was the fourth child. Grandmother Katie was a teacher and her husband John was the headmaster of the Catholic boys' primary school. They chose to stay on in Lisburn after the burnings in 1920. Katie's sisters, brothers, nieces and nephews, mostly business folk in the town, whose homes and shops were gutted beyond repair, all left to start a new life in Belfast or County Down.

I ask her: 'Why did you stay, Grandmother Katie, when all of your kin had gone and nothing was left in the town but emptiness and desolation?'

Turning her head back from the garden she answers: 'Your Grandfather wouldn't leave. It behoved him to stay with his vocation. To be a teacher to the young people of Lisburn. He taught sums and reading to all the children around us no matter their religion. That didn't change after the burnings, but it took us a while to regain our footing.'

I say to her: 'It's not the first time a family was sacrificed for a noble aim. How you lived through those decades afterwards I will never know.'

Katie replies: 'Indeed, but I agreed with him and passed this noble aim on to my children dearest, one and all.'

I tell her: 'Bright sparks they were, your children, sons and daughters all. That light spilled into all their work of teaching and sports and Gaelic culture. Good work was done, there's no denying, and proud you were of all of them. But what of human hearts therein, that in that town became scarred and thin? And underneath their spirits bright was a haunting hard to miss. A legacy deep of shame and fear. I saw it in their faces, those children of yours, who were kinfolk of mine.'

'Music, drama and the songs,' she says, 'kept us buoyant, alive and strong in the years thereafter, when darker days became the norm. You've no idea,' she adds, shaking her head, 'what we lived with for years after that. All across this Northern land, on both sides of the religious divide, it was a time of survival. Everything around was tense. But that is all water under the bridge. Those times are past us now and things are changing in your lifetime.'

'Indeed they are,' I say, 'and you long dead. But patterns still remain in families right across this land where women's pain is deep. The price they paid was much too high. And children's hearts were crushed, while sharp-tongued mothers said too much, their own loss never healed.

'These last words I say to you, Grandmother Katie. Much change has come in these few years, it'll be your heart's delight to know. The fruits of folk's good work in that town have cast a heavy tyranny down. Please know my call to help to heal the family soul within us all. And I will keep on going there with questions, songs and prayers for all. With this kind talk, I say goodbye to you and them and all for now.'

I breathe a sigh with a word of farewell: 'When such healing might take place in the soul of this town, perhaps we could imagine Macha coming to sit with us in Lisburn's Market Square, holding her wildness around her like the fresh breeze of the ocean. We would simply watch, with grace and ease, the women of the town pass by.'

'A picture of hope,' my Grandmother says and laughs a hearty laugh.

I smile at her and I know that this will be the end of our shared words across the veils of time and place and history. The work is done and we can rest.

God bless you, Grandmother dear.

April 2001, Cruit Island

Seven women gather at dusk to draw a large map of Ireland in the sand on the beach. We put crystals over the four provinces of Ireland: Munster, Leinster, Connaught and

Ulster. We put one in the mythical centre of the land to represent the Hill of Uisneach. Another two are placed for the heavenly bodies – the Moon and Sun. It is a Rose Quartz that is placed over Ulster.

We bring the Map alive with songs, allowing the crystals to harmonise with the chunky, pink granite that is the local rock here. As the light fades, big hulks of this native stone become rounded sentinels on all sides of us, guarding the beach.

Carefully calculating the time of high tide, I return at 4.30 in the morning to pick up the crystals, but the sea has already covered most of the map.

'How can this be?' I ask, scrambling along the sand to find the crystals. All are gone except the Rose Quartz placed over Ulster. I let go, and sit a long time in silence as the tide advances up the beach, more and more each minute. The waves are huge and move rapidly across the shore in large circles. Pushing up, turning around, streaming sideways. The sound of them is uncanny, almost frightening.

An hour later, the women join me. They are smiling when I tell them the crystals are gone and they begin to dance. In the pre-dawn light, I see the dark outlines of them spreading out along the beach. The white water is relentlessly streaming upwards. I follow the trails of surf along the beach. Both high tide and dawn are an hour away.

'The waves coming in are like bear paws,' one of the women says. Ah ... I start to see ... the foaming waves leave tracks that look exactly like bear paws fanning out on the shore. It was Bear Mother who took the crystals into the sea in the early hours of this morning. Leaving her mark on this place and on our work. I begin to thaw.

I hear these words as I move back into the myth: 'I took the whole Map,' Bear Mother is saying, 'the crystals, a part of it all. They will go on working their magic, bringing healing and balance to your land. I left you the Rose Quartz that was placed over the North, so you would know it was my paws that spread those huge and unexpected waves across the shore in the darkest hours before the dawn. It was not a wild and unpredictable sea coming in to destroy all that you had worked for.

'I took Ireland out beyond the ninth wave, and there she will be purified, cleansed and made new. In this realm, where the Dé Danann dwell, the spirit of the land will be rebirthed. The power of ancient alignments, reawakened.'

CHAPTER FIVE
Child of Lisburn

A little girl's presence
Is skipping along beside me.
She is playing a game
Of jumping from dry patch to dry patch.
Laughing.

December 1995, Lisburn

Thirty years ago, in the early 1960s,
A little five-year-old girl walked home alone
Through the streets of Lisburn,
From her primary school in Seymour Street
To her home on the Antrim Road,
A distance of over a mile.
A mother gave permission.
She said yes to this little girl,
Who asked for the independence and freedom
To walk home by herself.
Unknown to the little girl,
A brother followed on a bicycle
A distance behind her,
To make sure she was safe
At the traffic lights and road crossings.
A mother trusted this warrior girl
To find her way home alone,
Risking that her own
Small strength and confidence
Was enough to navigate such a task.

There is a park in Lisburn town called after Richard Wallace. He was the resident landlord in the late 1800s who granted the town sixteen acres of land for a park. Lisburn, located on the banks of the River Lagan, was a thriving market town in those days and a most prosperous centre of linen manufacturing.

Trees were planted throughout the park and avenues laid along it. Neat, red-bricked gate lodges guarded each entrance. The gates on the western side led out across to the railway station. On the eastern side, the gates faced towards Hilden and the Low Road, where the linen factories were. To the north was a large circular ring fort and the railway line ran along the southern boundary. A bandstand was positioned just off the main avenue, allowing people to sit and listen to what music might be performed there.

Completed in 1885, the lines and design of Wallace Park were beautifully proportioned. It became a pride and joy within the town. An elegant place for relaxation and recreation or perambulation to take the air.[1]

The overall form of this space still holds the grace and dignity of its original intention: to be there for the health and wellbeing of the people of Lisburn. Extended to twenty-five acres in later years, it was, within the structure of the town, a place set apart and remains so to this day.

All of the trees in the park are special. Many of the original trees stand alongside some new ones. Trees overhang the wide walkways and their rustic leaves fill the paths in the autumn. Other trees are spaced out singly across the parkland. A very old hawthorn stands in the centre of the grass close to the neatly trimmed rose beds.

On the path curving upwards to the duck pond there are tall trees of oak and beech, the girths of which are wide enough to suggest that they have shed their leaves, year in and year out, at least a hundred times.

If trees could speak, what stories would they tell of Lisburn over a hundred years? Would the trees remember the kindness of their benefactor who was known to take delight in giving to the people of this town? Would the trees recall the games of cricket and tennis played in this park over many generations? Or the boys who rolled up their shirt sleeves to play handball at the alley wall? Would they have seen the colourful dresses of the little girls on the swings and seesaws?

~

It is Christmas Eve morning in December 1995. I am wheeling my father through Wallace Park. He had a stroke and since an operation in October he is no longer able to walk. I am in awe as I push the wheelchair along the paths that, even in his debilitated place, he still greets all the people we meet along the way with civility and respect. From the cheerful drunk with a turquoise shirt, sprawled on a bench, to the family with children coming in to play, he greets them all alike.

This morning I am thinking of my Northern Irish soul and the 'Ulster Otherworld'. It is the first time I realise that the Ulster Otherworld is Macha's world. It is a different entity from the Celtic mystical Otherworld of the west. It is earthy, sensate, full of fun and down-to-earth passion and good humour. And I realise that all through my childhood, my father kept the door of this Otherworld open to us. We were, as children, brought into the mythic magic of a world beyond the North's six-county separation.

And even though the feminine was repressed in his family, due in part to their Catholic religion, as we connect to this light here today I see a resonance in my father's work in Lisburn and my work in Galway and the Aran Islands. Today, I see the park as a public place in this town and am aware of its connection to nature. I realise that the trees here are healing trees. This is a revelation. The light of the Ulster soul is very much with us today as I sing to my father and he, barely able to talk, is singing back to me.

At the end of this special morning, I have glimpsed a bigger picture. A deeper understanding of what held my father here and the path his life took. He had a great love for this town. It shows in how he moves through it, how people respond to him. His life was devoted to living here and being a teacher in a school in the rural hinterland. At the heart of all of that was his love of music, song and story.

I would have much preferred if we had been reared in

the wilds of north Antrim with my mother's people, but this morning is a moment of seeing beyond all of this. A month ago, I changed my married surname back to my original family name.

I am pushing your wheelchair
Through the park in Lisburn.
It is Christmas Eve,
I am singing.
You sing, too,
In a squeaky voice that is of another world.
I am weeping.
I watch the way you greet strangers,
As you always did,
With a generous heart.
The guy on the bench, with a few bottles of beer
Waves a greeting, and you,
Barely able to talk, you say hello.
To the old couple walking their dog,
You salute with the hand that still moves.
For you are at home here, Dad,
In a way that I never was.
As I am walking,
I am struck with inspiration.
In this moment it is given to me
To see beyond the things
That I have long since rejected in your life,
Patriarchal, Catholic structures,
Masculine values in a Protestant town,
To the light of the Irish soul
That truly inspired you.
Remembering you when you were well,
Smiling and laughing, telling stories.
I can see that light in your eyes,
Organising as you did,

Music concerts, drama and the Féis.
With these new thoughts about you,
I am singing again
And still pushing you along, uphill now,
To the duck pond.
I, too, have a sense of calling
To keep the Irish soul
Alive in barren places,
Like Lisburn or the Aran Islands.
I come back home to your name, Dad.

CHAPTER SIX
Healing Peace

Visualise a golden light
In your heart,
Grounding it in your body.
Green Isle,
Deep heart chakra,
Golden Irish,
Fairy gold,
Mythical.
Deepest possibility
Of forgiveness.

June 2010, Derry to Ohio

It is 7.00am on the first Tuesday in June 2010. Dressed in a coloured skirt of bright pink, orange and black and a green cardigan, I am standing at the bus stop outside the shopping centre on Strand Road in Derry. Later this morning I will fly out of Belfast International, bound for Newark, en route for Cincinnati. It is a dull morning, but not cold. At this early hour there is an empty silence in the city. I pull on a raincoat to keep out the damp air.

I have been invited to an International Peace Gathering at Hope Springs Institute, a retreat and learning centre in Ohio.[1] I have visited there often and given workshops and was a founding member of the Board. But this is a different challenge – to deliver a keynote presentation on the theme of *Healing Peace in Northern Ireland*. I will be there for a while beforehand and will spend the mornings walking the land, sitting in silence and gathering my notes to design a structure for this talk. A colleague is also coming over from Ireland and he will help me with the preparation.

A week later, I am at the podium facing an audience of over seventy people. Dressed in a beautiful green skirt and white top, with a pale-coloured batik scarf around my shoulders, I have called in the presence of the Tuatha Dé Danann to assist with the flow of this presentation. My fiddle is on a table in front of me and the script is carefully arranged on the wooden stand beside me. I walk around the space gathering power and sensing the right moment to begin:

This is a story of the heart. The heart of Ireland. The heart of the land. The heart of history. A lot of what has happened in Ireland is about betrayal. It was betrayal on many levels and dimensions. Of people. Of places. Of land and soul.

Over the centuries, there has been loss and shock and more layers of betrayal. And, as the old patterns of war are receding now, many people in the North of Ireland are coming into a new place. We want a fresh start. To leave the bigotry behind. Move on from the rage. Release the fear that is binding people to the past.

Healing the heart is a journey of releasing old hurts. The journey now is to move beyond the divisions of north and south. Beyond Catholic and Protestant, rich and poor, us and them. For every person it is a healing of their own heart and the heart of their family line. Tremendous courage has been shown by people in Ireland to face the past and let it go. The mending of all has been continuing over many years in communities across the North. People are ready to forgive.

This story is also about Rose Quartz. As crystals for healing the heart, they can help with the release of the wounding. I have used them on many occasions to assist in the work I have done over these years. The Rose Quartz here on the table (a tall angular-shaped piece of pink rock) is one that I purchased in the Rock Shop in County Clare some years ago. I have brought it for this presentation and will leave it at Hope Springs to support the ongoing vision of peace and tolerance that everyone here is working towards in their own lives.

It is a privilege to be here and share some of my journey of healing in the North of Ireland. I dedicate this story for release and healing for all of us here in this room today. As we sit and bear witness to each other, may we allow the old patterns to be shed. Let go of those scripts that we hold in our heads that continue to wound us. May we expand our hearts and breathe in a new light for the future. Thank you for being here, and for what each of you do in your own communities, to help us to move towards peace in this world.

When I have finished the opening speech, I take up my fiddle and play. From here, the stories flow: the history that has impacted events in Ireland, the beauty of the land, the magic of the myths and the journeys of healing. I recount the drama of Macha lifting her curse in Glenties and share the beauty of all the workshops with people in the North and the magic of the light of crystals moving across the song lines of the world.

July 2012, Moville

It is July 2012, a few weeks after the last conversation with my Grandmother as she sat in the kitchen looking out at the garden. Today, in my upstairs study in Moville, I sense a spirit presence coming in to speak with me. It is my Granda John. I am surprised. In all my years I have not met his spirit often. I do recall one occasion, an afternoon in March 2009, when he made his presence felt, the very week that Pearse Lawlor launched his book *The Burnings 1920*.[2] We agreed then, my Granda and I, that there is a thick vein of misogyny running through the whole culture of Northern Ireland in both men and women.

Today, Granda is saying: 'Thank you for the work you have done for all of us. You have helped to heal so much of what was lost. Yes, we were wounded by the discrimination and the burnings in Lisburn. But it was my choice to stay, to keep my family there, to continue in a life of dedication and purpose to educate Catholic people. I wanted not to leave that. But a stubborn man I was and life might have been easier for all of us had we gone to a kinder place to rear our six children.

'Katie's heart was broken when her own family left the town. She was a tough woman and she never said a word about it. But there were no longer any sisters and brothers living in the town for us to call in to for a cup of tea, nor any relations who would walk up to us for a visit. Nor were there cousins for the children to go and play with.'

As he is recounting the pain of those years, I am thinking of what it cost them to stay in Lisburn, to become who they were within that community. A litany of damage was done in Ulster in the early 1900s. The words come back to me: *Damage so deep, how would you ever get to the bottom of it?*

He continues: 'I acknowledge the work my children did in the years after that. There is no doubt their work brought light to people there. They were good teachers and leaders in the community. I am proud of all they did. But I am sorry for the price we all paid for my stubbornness. For the pain I caused to my family. Especially to my daughters.

'I set harsh rules. I believed that the strictness and severity was a necessary protection to survive in the alien environment around us. But it was a closing of our hearts. The fear that made us keep our heads down. The shame we could never fully shake. We shut ourselves off from the hurt of it. No tears were allowed in the house. We took on an air of proud reserve to protect ourselves from all of it.'

I hear myself saying the words of Macha's song from the Aran Islands: *I will hold your daughters in my arms, Granda John. I will hold your daughters in my arms.* As I think of my three aunts, I remember a dark night on the shore of Inis Mór, at Samhain time in October 1992, and the words that were said to me then: *They have their own story, the women in your family line who have gone before.*

I take a deep breath, momentarily closing my eyes with the memory of that night. Granda continues: 'The choice of response is always our own. And the consequences of the choice to remain there belong to me and to no-one else. I cannot blame the men who created the Orange state for the severity I imposed on my own family in order to survive in that life. I cannot blame the Unionist politicians who blocked the funding to Catholic schools for the isolation I created in my own children.'[3]

As Granda John continues to speak, I hear the words from the hill in Glenties echoing in my ears: *The harsh cruel hardness of the men of Ulster*, coming all the way through the years from that rain-drenched night in 1999 when Macha lifted her curse. I am thinking as I listen to Granda: *The harshness that was needed to protect vulnerable truth.*

And, as I weep the tears that were never shed by him or Katie or their children, I know that the soft rain from the hill in Glenties continues to dissolve the 'harsh cruel hardness' of the men of Ulster. My Granda John, who lived in Lisburn in those punishing times of the early 1900s, is yet another man, amongst all the men of Ulster, now releasing himself from Macha's curse.

It is Macha who says: 'It is the tears that will dissolve the pain and bring kindness back into the heart of Ulster. Tears that weren't shed for decades afterwards. The cruelty of what they all lived in. The cold, bitter emptiness of it. Tell the stories. Cry the tears. Release the pain. Move on.'

I look out the back window. A magpie is sitting on a fence post. And in the field beyond, a soft wind moves across the fresh growth of barley, creating rivers of shimmering green.

A year from now, in August 2013, I will go in a brightly patterned summer skirt and sit with Macha outside a cafe in Lisburn's Market Square. Grandmother Katie's spirit will be well gone from the story by then. Macha and I will recall the places where Katie's family had business premises. As we sit, we will hold the grace of feminine light and watch the women of the town pass by.

I will then go to the graveyard in Lisburn where my Grandparents are buried alongside some of their children.

My father's remains are in a plot beside them along with those of my mother. I will pull out the weeds and then pick wild geraniums, lavender and a rose from a flower garden in the car park and put them on the grave.

I will stand and watch as hundreds of starlings fly over and back across the sky above me. They will continue this rapid dance, making a cutting sound with the slash of their wings. Over and back, over and back. Some ten minutes later, they will spread out and fly away in the direction of White Mountain, a hill to the north of the town. I will hear these words:

Release the doves of peace.
The colour of forgiveness
Is the rich ruby red
Of the King Joy lily,
That is flowering in your front garden.

CHAPTER SEVEN
Music with the Men of Ulster

All of a sudden, the whole place is quiet.
A strange eerie silence has descended.
We know something has changed.
You can feel it in the air:
Lighter ... Stronger ... Otherworldly.
And then the Great Macha
Steps towards all of us,
Her anger spent.
She speaks softly and gently:
'You are forgiven, men of Ulster,
The curse of Macha will be no more.'

July 2012, Donegal

It is Captain's Night at Greencastle Golf Club. Many are gathered for an evening of celebration. There will be prizes for games. Speeches and recognition will accompany the presentations. Good food and wine will be served in a marquee outside. We will play music to bring cheer to people on this summer evening, bright still, as the late sun hangs mellow in the sky over the waters of Lough Foyle.

Wearing a summer skirt of bright pink and blue, I carry in my violin case and take a seat at a table close to the window. My face is alive with the sun-reddened tan built up from many days outside at the sea and in the garden. Since the conversations with my Grandparents across the veils of the spirit world, a brightness has returned to my own spirit that had been missing for many months. As each of my music companions comes in, we move tables and chairs to give us space to play. We corner off an area at the window beside the piano. Seven of us take our seats around the tables, and as we sit chatting and tuning our instruments, I look around to get a sense of our audience.

There must be over a hundred golfers here tonight, invited for this event from clubs all over Northern Ireland. Many from Antrim and Down are work colleagues of the captain's. They have come along with women and children, wives and grandmothers. The men are dressed in crisp summer shirts and smart trousers. The women are wearing stylish dresses of bright colours. The children run back and forth to their tables, taking sips of drinks.

Fascinated by this whole scene, I watch the visiting men with a great curiosity. As golfers and Ulstermen, they remind me of the men we encountered in the Highlands Hotel in Glenties during our pilgrimage of 1998. Isn't it strange the way things change over time? I recall the way the autumn evening sunlight lit up the tans of those men's faces as they filed into the private dining room in the hotel. Similar to that, the summer-tanned look of the golfers here tonight. As they walk by and greet each other, their banter is that same quick wit of Northern Irish men. As they gradually settle into their seats having ordered drinks, I see their instant camaraderie.

Amused to find myself in the midst of this gathering, I look over at my music companions, mostly golfers and men from the North themselves. Chatting now and cracking jokes as part of warming up, they catch the smile on my face, filled with excitement and delight. I join in the banter and they tell me who is going to win the prizes. I catch a glimpse of two prize-winning lady golfers who, dressed in smart outfits, are brimming with pride. An air of achievement radiates from them.

The captain is circulating. A tall, handsome man with a boyish face. Indeed, in a kilt, he would pass for a Gaelic prince, he has that kind of strident confidence and air of gentle sovereignty. Attentive to us, he ensures we have enough to drink. Bringing me a glass of wine, he points the way to the food marquee outside and thanks us all in advance for the music.

After tuning our instruments we begin to play. Taking our time to warm up against the bustle and noise of so many people, we work hard to bring in that spark of magic that will lift the energy of this evening from its own dull self-importance. In those beginning moments, what is it that holds the energy down? Is it the resistance of so many in a tight space? This is not the talk that comes from the heart. This is the talk of men that pins down the energy of soul. Refuses to meet the eye of the music and let it sing. This is the force that Macha has been challenging in Ulster for all these years. A wall that is hard to compete with.

Yet, within it all, there seems to be a hunger for something. Connection, laughter, a question vibrating underneath the surface: *Can we tolerate the silence for enough time to let the music touch us? What will it be, men of Ulster? Will you give way soon?* I wonder. *Or will we be fighting an uphill struggle all evening?*

We hold the tension of this for almost an hour.

As the music continues, we have created a strength of beat and a unity of purpose. My body is pulsing and as I close my eyes, I see another picture within this one.

I hear the sound of thundering hooves outside. When I look out the window, I see a herd of horses galloping across the fairways, between us and the sea. Three have stopped and are looking in the window. A grey face speckled with white is pushing her head against a brown face and black mane. A third, a chestnut with a rust mane, is whinnying and dancing. I sense a different energy enter the room. I look down at my feet moving with the beat of the music. I see another foot beside mine. Or is it a hoof?

I turn and, with a start, see Macha sitting beside me, smiling. Called in by the sheer power of our playing, she has entered the room. She is tapping her foot on the floor. She winks at me and, as the music dances on, I sense the light and strength of the Ulster soul coming in to join us. I look out the window just in time to see the three horses lift their heads, whinny at us and then gallop off, back to join the herd.

Macha's face is shapeshifting back and forth to that of a beautiful mare. She is wearing a dress of royal blue with threads of silver through it and her dark hair is wet from rain. I smell wood smoke from her. I am puzzled at first and then it dawns on me. Glenties! The hill and the healing we did. The night we lifted the curse. The images flash before me: I see the faces of the women from Arizona and from Ireland lit up by the light of the fire. I see the warriors on their knees, speaking to Macha. I sense her powerful presence. She is telling them to get off their knees and stand up straight.

I look again at Macha here beside me tonight as I play music in Greencastle. She is looking around at the gathering of golfers and is evidently amused with it all.

'You lifted the curse that night in Glenties, Macha.'

'Yes,' she says, 'and this night I am here to celebrate with you and them,' she nods towards my music companions, 'the healing of the men of Ulster.' Macha turns round to me and continues: 'Child of Lisburn, do you think things have changed since we lifted the curse? Are the battles over now?'

As I look around, everyone's face has become a horse's head neighing and snorting to each other. The whole room is alive with the vibrant energy of 'horse soul'. Shaking my head in disbelief, I see the faces around me soften. A glow of light has come into the room. Pure feminine light. The place has become quieter and the hush allows the music to be heard. We musicians all sense the change and nod at one another. We can step up the tempo. We have the audience with us at last.

As I whizz through the tunes, my arms and fingers are moving fast. Songs are spun out with feeling and passion from the men around me. We are connecting in harmony. With skill and precision, we are weaving a flow and bouncing off each other's rhythm. There is a counterpoint of magic within each beat.

As we continue, tune after tune, my fiddle is dancing, my eyes, sparkling. We are flowing brilliantly now and with great ease. I catch the eye of a man across the room. He is smiling with appreciation. An Ulsterman who lives locally, he has a rich sense of soul. He has been connecting with us from the beginning. In every song and tune. As I smile back at him, my heart fills with joy, and, in the holding of a new, soft, truth, in some very lovely way, this exchange carries the beauty of the healed Ulster soul. Like the spark that brings new love to life, we are all children of the stars.

As songs are sung by all, the light of fairy music filters into our midst. The reality of witnessing a curse of ages lifted from the shadows of men and women. Tonight, I come home to a forgotten heritage. The beauty and passion and deep felt joy of the Ulster soul. Women and men, together, celebrating a new dawn. I belong with all of them.

I notice at the top of the room both the captain and the Master of Ceremonies are making subtle signs at us to stop playing, impatient to get on with the speeches and prize giving. Caught up in the hypnotic beat of a final tune, we make instantaneous eye contact across our circle. We rebel against this force upon us. Our spirits bounce off it. We bridle against being reined in and the voice of the music is saying: *Don't dare touch us here!*

I glance up from my fiddle playing as Macha says to me: 'Do you think he would dance with me, that handsome Gaelic prince?' And, without waiting for an answer, she gets up and moves to the middle of the room. She takes the captain by the arm. He takes a few faltering steps. It would be hard to resist the force of Macha's power. Suddenly, his body has burst into a wild jig. His feet are moving so fast you cannot see them! I turn back to the music, smiling broadly and, in an unforgettable surge of power, we play on and on ... into the wildness of this night's Dervish Dance. For here ... for us ... for all ...

> *Those were the days, my friend,*
> *We thought they'd never end,*
> *We'd sing and dance forever and a day.*
> *We'd live the life we choose,*
> *We'd fight and never lose,*
> *For we were young,*
> *And sure to have our way.*[1]

∼

On the first Monday in August 2012, in the season of Lúghnasa², I am gardening out at the little house at Tirrion. It is a dull day. I light a fire to burn the stalks of the early potatoes. July was so wet it brought the blight. I stand back and watch for a while as smoke billows out and wood crackles. I am waiting for that moment when flames will burst forth within it. I can hear the dancing feet of the ancestor people from generations past, building strength as they send their grief and their prayers into the earth.

The fire pushes upwards and the leaves on the top burn clean in these flames. The fire is giving out an ethereal blue-coloured smoke that dances and swirls up and out through the trees, filling the old yard with an otherworldly light. I sit in silence and watch the movement of this smoke. It is cleansing everything in its path.

Several hours later, when every piece of old stalk is burned, I take the last small pile of smouldering wood ash and scatter it between the rows of the new potato plants. I say a prayer with this offering: 'May there be no more blight on these lands.'

The following Friday is a rich and beautiful day. My gardening friend, Peter, and I are fixing the fence on the seaward boundary. A breeze from the ocean keeps us cool as we work. I stop for a moment to look around me, hands leaning on the spade as I take time to survey the land.

It is glorious today in the heat of summer. Fresh green grass shimmers in the sun, whilst the leaves of the trees rustle in the warm breeze. As the fresh fragrance of fluffy, cream meadowsweet wafts around us, I recall the commitment I made at the winter solstice of 2008 when we first placed the boundaries of my site here at Tirrion. Almost four years now and, with Peter's help, I have consistently tended the land. Planting trees, chopping windfall wood and trimming bushes. Tidying the paths at the lane and growing vegetables in the garden at the little house. There are posts still marking the outline of the house. So hard to leave this place. A love so pure. A healing so deep.

The next day I go out again to the land and walk down the slope of the hill. Another bright, beautiful day. I am admiring the new sections of the fence. At the bottom of the site, I lie on the grass, resting deeply. Held here in a great sense of contentment. To be in communion with your deepest self and with the core essence of everything around you is a gift given from the land to me today.

I sense in this place of heightened awareness that the patterns of Church oppression and shame, held in the memory of this glen, are finally clearing. With the power of renewal and the land's own life force, the sensual beauty of nature is free to dance again in the summer sun.

A few days later, ten healers come to a meditation at the little house at Tirrion. A celebration evening for Lúghnasa.

They arrive with smiling faces and expectation. Each person enters with a gift of abundance to put on the altar to celebrate the *Fruits of the Harvest*.[3] Some sit on chairs and others settle on cushions on the floor. The place is alive with the rich colours of summer fruits and flowers, home-baked breads and sweet-smelling cakes. The room is filling with an evening summer light that is warming the hearts of all. Chatter dies down and we begin our meditation. Each person is quietly guided to enter the silence: 'Breathe in to deepen and relax. Breathe out to release. Hold in stillness. What is it you are releasing? What are you harvesting?'

I sense the spirit of the harvest come into the room. It brings in a light, the colour of golden corn, and assists each person to enter more deeply into their own essence. I look around at the folk gathered here with their faces in quiet contemplation. I breathe in, with my own sense of relief for work well done and to celebrate a year of healing on this land at Tirrion.

As people emerge slowly from their quiet space of inner reflection, I take up my fiddle and play a slow jig to close. I sense the sparkling magic of the fairy folk gathering around the house. They are giving their blessing to all here. The joy of their return is held in the heart of the land now. A harmony restored and mirrored in the healers gathered here. I see the magic of each person present adding to the dance that is bubbling beneath the surface.

The kettle is put on for tea. Slices of cake and bread are cut and buttered. Laughter and good cheer erupts as we open the door and spill out into the garden where pink roses and the small purple flowers known as 'self-heal' are growing. I sense the child in each of us is ready to dance again. Most of us present here tonight were, as children, reared within the six counties of Northern Ireland. With this common history, we glimpse the possibilities of new times to come. Gifted healers who will meet again many times, bringing their skills to mend the past. Dancing all eventually to freedom.

PART III
Joy

CHAPTER EIGHT
Autumn Peace

Autumn Peace is the time in our story
When the healing is done on many levels
And a quiet knowing of completion
Begins to settle in the soul.
The softness of the young feminine
Is able to blossom and thrive,
Bringing its fragile light to everything around.

October 2012, Tirrion

On a Tuesday morning in early October, I am working out at the little house. I take time to go outside and walk down the lane. I know at this time of autumn light that the 'famine fires' that burned in August represent the final vestiges of the shadow and loss that were ready to be cleared across this valley in Donegal.

When I stand at the gate to the yard on this calm morning and listen carefully as the soft sun slips through the trees, I feel the presence of the ancestors, with no trace of their sorrow. There is a quiet abiding peace here in the new light given in a year of deep transforming release. I sigh outwardly, looking at the last few brown and yellow leaves dangling on the trees in the yard. Tears trickle down my cheeks in gratitude and relief.

My brother died at the end of the summer. I mourn him deeply this autumn, the loss of him sore in my whole being. Unbearable to face. 'John is gone. Our lovely John is gone.' I say it over and over again as if some day I might believe it.

Through my tears, and in my silent contemplation, I hear the spirits of this land of Tirrion speaking to me: 'Come out to the little house and abide with us for the winter. The light here will hold you. And in the stillness of this season, your soul will be cleansed and eased. When springtime comes around anew, you can begin again to live and love.'

November 2012

It is the last week of the month. On each day of this special week I have conversations with four girls and young women aged from nine to thirty-three. The vibrancy of each of them resonates across the distances I travel – from Sligo to Dublin and back to Sligo again.

I held each of these girls in my arms when they were

babies and have watched them all as they have grown up. Babies to little girls, young girls to women. Each blossoming as the wheel turns to new stages of their lives. As they engage with life's challenges, I see them tested and honed, new each year. I witness them growing into the confidence and power of their own magnificent spirits.

On Monday, in a house in Sligo town, I am at a kitchen table being served lunch. The young woman across from me has long dark hair tied back and perched high on her head. Her brown eyes, almost oriental in their depth, hold me in a strong, steady gaze. At twenty-one, she is considering choices of career: *What course to follow now? Where to take direction from? What is important in all of it?* We discuss possibilities as we eat, exchanging ideas and looking at options. As she gets up to make us tea, I ponder the years since I was twenty-one and all the things I did with my life. *What process had I used to guide me? And whose advice did I seek, or even listen to?*

She is very capable. A woman of great integrity, solid intelligence. The kindest girl you could ever meet. At eight years old she was able to make tea for visitors.

I sip from my cup and ask: 'What is in your heart? For that is where you must go to find a true answer. That choice will guide your compass and always take you home.'

She nods. She knows.

On Tuesday, I sit in a coffee bar in Dublin with another young woman. Muffled up in winter hats and scarves, we peel off layers and sit on high stools facing each other. It is late afternoon and dusk is approaching. We both order a latte. She, too, has long dark hair and bright eyes. Her smile is open and wide, warm. She has the kind of luminous glow that softens a room into which she walks. There is a generous sensibility about her. This woman is thirty-three.

Hands folded around the hot mugs to keep warm, we speak of matters of life and love. Of challenge and loss.

How the deepest truths of life are slowly revealed as we move forward. Her lovely brown eyes meet mine and swim with tears as she grapples with the lessons flung out on life's journey. Our hands reach out across the table to grasp and reassure.

On Wednesday, in north Sligo, I am in a sitting room with two young girls who sprawl across a sofa. Both are wrapped up in blankets, off school with winter colds. One is a girl of thirteen years. Her light brown hair is long and thick, falling loosely about her shoulders. Her face is strong with the translucent glow of a pale English rose. Her mouth is the shape of a butterfly, perfectly formed and full. Poised, she is ready to bring to life any topic of conversation that is put on the table.

Her sister of nine years is a small girl, willowy and fine. Her fair hair is long and straight and neatly frames her face. Wise beyond her years, her light brown eyes move quickly with a flash of starlight in their knowing. She is a girl who sees the hidden forms and patterns of many things. A hugeness in her universal soul.

Chatting as we go, of school and pals, games and news, I hear all the things they have done in the past week. Tales of the girls and boys who people their worlds at school. Later in the day, we tell stories of ships wrecked at sea. Pirate raids where gold and silver are taken in the night. Ferried up the channel and out to sea.

On Thursday, the younger girl stays at home again. She stands up straight in front of the kitchen bench and chirps out the notes of *The Little Drummer Boy*[i] on her tin whistle. I keep time with my foot and sing the words along with her.

I recall myself at nine years old. Putting the notes of songs together and learning how to grasp my violin bow with gentleness so as not to scrape and scratch. As these deep days of November draw to a close, the spirit of Christmas is coming in, slowly, to brighten us.

At the end of the week, as I drive back to Donegal, I hear Macha's voice saying to me: *It is important to witness the blossoming of the young feminine. This has been a special week. These girls are all a part of our story.*

December 2012

I stay out at the little house at Tirrion for the winter, as the spirits of the land advised. I sleep at night with an open window and, as the year comes to a close, I come home to myself.

Last week the waxing moon shone brightly, touching my heart. It gave me dreams of sparkling magic that left my whole body awash with a healing glow. The wind whipped in and around me, touching my face with a cooling caress. Nights of clear skies, with moonlight bearing down on me as I slept. Magical, intense and beautiful.

Last night I heard the heavy rain outside. The elements are washing my soul clean.

I go to the beach each morning. First footprints on sand that has been washed by the heavy rains and scoured clean by the night-time tides that are rising to meet the moon in her fullness. Today, I walk along the water's edge, marvelling as always at the colour and the animal shapes of the rocks. One is like a bear. Another two are like dolphins at the sea's edge. I watch the patterns of the sea swirling in and around them, rushing back out again to join the foam of the next wave surging in.

I find a sheltered place to stand at the edge of the waves and perform my T'ai Chi. I rub my hands to keep them warm on this bitter cold morning. As I complete the form and have reached that place of time slowing down, I sense Macha's presence beside the shining grey rocks and the cold, green-coloured waves of the sea. She is telling me: 'Our story is almost done now. Of Ulster and land. Of women and girls. Healing and soul. Rest well, Daughter, rest well.'

While I sit at my table by the window after the walk and craft some words, I am compelled to stop and stand. I take my drum and begin to play to a rhythm I hear in the air.

The power in the glen is tangible today. A gathering of many can be felt. I sense the spirits of horses again. Bright sun a few days ago. Water in floods today around the lanes. Fire, earth, water and air, all holding strong. In the short hours of daytime, a mist hangs low in that strange half-light of a winter afternoon. I dance with all the spirits who have resided in the mythic soul of this land since we first began to tell the story. I celebrate with them the freedom and the fragile new light that is holding solid, here in the heart of the glen.

The following morning I go for a walk up the steep 'high lane' that leads to the turf bogs. The air is cold and raw and the rain is biting against my cheeks. I pick my steps alongside a stream that is running down the middle of the track. I breathe deeply. It is good to be out. Last night I dreamt that we, as women, are constantly moving in and out of being girls as well. This flow is part of our nature. All our lives we hold the girl within us.

I notice stones of white quartz glistening under the water. All different shapes and sizes embedded in the lane. In an instant, I am transported into the running stream and a vision opens up. I am a salmon swimming upriver, against the flow, to the place where I was spawned. I, too, will leave my eggs there for hatching and new life.

The images swirl and disappear. Another picture forms as I travel into the heart of the white stones on the lane. The quartzite rock opens itself to reveal the memory held within it.

I see images of the feet of every woman who has ever walked up this track over generations. Those who herded cattle, prodding them on with an old blunt stick. The ones who pushed up at a stronger pace with bags slung over their shoulders, heading up to save the turf laid out in rows on the soft peat ground at the top of the hill.

Coming back out of these places of inner vision, I blink several times and shift back to myself. I breathe deeply and pause to look out at the views across the sea to the north. Calm water stretches into nothingness, but I sense the expanse of miles beyond it, up towards Scotland and the Paps of Jura. Cold and uninviting, the rain is still pouring down.

Something is finding *me* now. I turn and sense the presence of Macha on the lane. I hear her speaking to me although I see nothing. Only her voice is clear, in answer to my question that I had not even realised I had asked: *Macha, how do I write the piece about girls and young women?*

She answers: 'This elemental raw wildness that you feel here today. This is the spirit within women that you want to speak of. It is a vitality of nature that flows onward like the stream of water on the lane. Nothing stops it. It is a raw life force.'

I turn to face into the wind and rain again. The mountain air clears my mind and lifts my whole being. I start to walk upwards towards the top of the hill, listening, as Macha continues to speak to me: 'Teach a young girl the truth about who she is. Let her be in the sheer power of her beauty and magic, wildness and strength. Witness her there and celebrate it. Let her experience the sheer physical pleasure of running across beaches, riding horses, climbing mountains.

'Honour the fact that young girls start to bleed and in the bleeding become young women. Help them to walk confidently over this threshold into womanhood and shed what they no longer need of childhood ways.

'Deepen their connection to nature. Teach them the cyclical rhythms inherent in their souls that reflect the moon's path each month, each year. The natural ebb and flow through fullness and blossoming, from winter's stillness to summer's fruits. Help them to learn the patience to gestate the new and how to use the life force in nature that keeps the body in harmony with all.

'A little girl who at seven can sing with the music of rivers and is nourished by the spirit of nature becomes at fourteen a young woman who can still benefit from a connection to nature's power. It will support her into the strength of physical boundaries. A girl thus nourished will have the authority of her own body and soul. Teach her how to use her female energy as a force for wellbeing and vitality, a sacred power for life and love. Guide her to choose companions and friends in a way that grows and strengthens her. Give her the freedom to do the dance of testing herself in the wider world, meeting the challenges and developing the confidence to find a path true to her heart. Celebrate with her a rite of passage where the old is shed and new robes put on.

'Help teenage girls to find themselves. Tell them the truth of whom they are and whom they can become, bringing forth new birth in all its forms to their families, communities and cultures. Show them how they can provide the wisdom, integrity and dignity to create a new world.'

After the walk on the hill, I come back to my house. I light a lavender candle to call in the power of Macha in her love and holding of young girls becoming women. As I lift up my drum and begin to sing, the pale winter sun brings in a stream of joy. I am remembering the week in November when I spent time with the girls and young women.

I join my voice today with the power of the Grandmothers of the land. I celebrate the radiant strength and beauty of each one of these four girls and young women and give thanks for their wisdom and light in the lives of all who love them.

I go to Lisburn to visit my friend Carol, an artist, who lives in Hilden where the linen mills thrived in earlier times. It is almost dusk. We go outside to her back garden and stand beside an apple tree.

My friend is quietly spoken. Serene and deeply thoughtful, her presence slows me down to a whisper. Then the whisper becomes my slow breathing as I find the deep connection with the earth here.

In the damp quiet of a winter afternoon I take out my fiddle. I play music to give thanks for everything that has been given by many people in the healing journey of this town. I play for the land both here in Antrim and there in Donegal. For Grandmother Katie and all her family, I offer my love. For the women who worked in the linen mills, I salute their courage. For the healers and artists who live here today, may their work be blessed. For all of the people who bring in kindness, I say: 'Thank you.'

I play for the trees in Wallace Park and for the children of the town yet to come. As the music flows out, I sense the soft delicate fragility of a returning light of the feminine stream in to join us, vulnerable and new. I play with quiet gratitude until there is nothing more except the presence of grace given.

On finishing, I reach down to touch the wet leaves underfoot. Quietly breathing, I am aware of the little girl within me whose presence has come to kneel down beside us. She pats the leaves into place as though reassuring the earth that the songs will stay there now. And she looks up at me with the brightest of smiles. I ask that the power of this music be carried out into the evening air and become an offering of peace. A prayer of thanks for everything.

CHAPTER NINE
Light of Brigid

Authentic feminine power
Is rooted in the wisdom of the physical body.
It rises from a deep well of wisdom within us
And is lifted into the realms of speech,
Where female voice can emerge.
Authentic female voice resonates in the collective soul,
Bringing to birth a new myth,
Of a healed and whole feminine spirit.
Through this we can join with the eternal patterns,
Unfolding in the cosmic universe.

February 2013, Armagh

Macha stands on the hill at Emain Macha and watches an incoming light. Her silent figure is strong and still. Dressed in a cloak of deep-blue velvet, her dark hair is wrapped in a scarf of blue and silver spirals. It is a year since the *Calling Macha Home* talk last Imbolc, when her wild spirit returned to Emain Macha. Today she is, once again, the sovereign Queen of Armagh at this ancient holy site of goddesses and warriors, waiting to welcome Brigid, the Goddess of spring.

In the weeks that I was preparing for a second talk at the Navan Centre in County Armagh, I saw Brigid draw a cloak of light right across the land of Ulster.

It began with a soft yellow glow emanating from Lough Neagh, the mythical lake. This light of Brigid was like a mist rising from within the waters, spreading outwards from the lake and easing into many pockets and places on the land.

I saw it sweeping like a wheel across the hills of Antrim, right up to the north coast and then, moving in waves westwards, it reached along the shores of Lough Foyle and back over towards the Sperrins in County Derry, spreading into the scenic hills of Tyrone. From there, it moved south to cover the lakes in Fermanagh and then circled across to County Armagh. Flowing over Down, this glow left a cloak of light over the Mourne Mountains and, finally, it moved northwards along the Ards Peninsula into Belfast Lough.

On Friday, 8 February 2013, an audience of some forty people have gathered at Emain Macha in County Armagh to listen to a presentation of the stories of Brigid, together with music, songs and poems. Some folk from last year are in the midst of this gathering tonight, and as they sit alongside the new faces, I sense Macha is pleased that they are here.

In the audience are three women who were at the Brigid weekend in Belfast in January 2000. As we sing the

Soulsmith Song from that gathering, we close the distance of those thirteen years and bring an energy of peace into the room tonight:

> *Brigid, you are guide of the women.*
> *Brigid, we are keepers of the flame.*
> *When we light the fires in Belfast*
> *We call the soul back home.*[1]

Brigid's presence is tangible in our midst. Carrying her spirit on the wind, Brigid, Celtic Mother Goddess and Saint, brings to all who might receive her light the qualities of truth, clarity, creativity and healing.

Tonight, we dare to call her 'Cosmic Brigid' and ask her to bring in an even higher light than heretofore. One that is linked to the sun and the moon and the stars, to all of the heavens above us.

We ask her: 'Will you assist us with Macha in the journey to restore a healed and whole feminine light back into the heart of Ulster?'

I look around the people with their faces lit up in the excitement of our evening. I sense the beauty of this moment sparkling in the air and how special it is to have Brigid's presence here at Emain Macha tonight. I am knowing that another moment of mythic history has written itself here in the land of Armagh and in the soul of this gathering.

> *An image of the dual feminine will be whole*
> *When Brigid and Macha meet again on sacred ground.*
> *Here, the light of the conscious feminine*
> *Will be joined with the wisdom of the wild,*
> *And a new archetype*
> *Of feminine spirituality*
> *Will emerge.*[2]

Some weeks after the talk on Brigid I am here at Tirrion to say my goodbyes to the land. It is the last Sunday in February and – recalling the words spoken by the spirits here last autumn: *When springtime comes, begin again to live and love* – I now know that I will not be living here or building a house on this site.

I lie in the hollow at the base of Sycamore Mother on a bank above the river. I hear Brigid say: 'The light will be held here by the stones, the trees and all the invisible ones who live in this glen. The song of the river, the whistle of the wind across the hillside and the quiet, deep silence, will be here always. The weaving of the pieces within Macha's story will remain in the memory of this place, beyond the lifetimes of all.'

I say my goodbyes in quiet whispers of gratitude. And with soft tears, I turn my face upwards to the early spring sunshine, awaiting the call to begin anew.

A few days later, Peter and Liam, a shamanic colleague, join with me to take down the fence at the site where I was to build. We work steadily, taking staples out of the wooden posts, yard by yard, all the way down the hill; lifting the posts out and laying them flat on the ground, rolling the wire onto a larger length of pole.

As we stop to eat our lunch in the lower part of the site, we watch the silver gleam of the river as it meanders through the valley, shining in spring sunshine. Munching apples and sandwiches and chatting, there is amongst us three a reverence for the mystery of it all. The land's wisdom. Its journey with me. First calling me home to build. Now releasing me to go and find somewhere else. And yet the spirit of it is so strong today. I sense the heart of it is healed now and so, too, is my heart.

By the middle of the afternoon the posts are lying in piles

at intervals up the hillside. Carrying two at a time, I do the steep climb up and down at least twenty times in order to place them all in one pile on the laneway.

At the end of the day we pause and survey the work. Catching sight of the field completely cleared of the fence, the small tree enclosures and the markers for the house, takes my breath away. There is no sense of loss, just gratitude for all that was given. The soft whispering of the ancestors I have heard with us all day.

By the end of the afternoon, two hawks fly in circles above us over the trees and around the site. I knew they would come to give their blessing for this final release. I watch them with a sense of awe, remembering the journey through these five years, each step of which is vivid today. A glow is spreading across everything here, a silver light and a starlight blessing. A sense of heaven on earth. You would remember a day like this for the rest of your life.

CHAPTER TEN
Angels in Belfast

When you look through soft eyes
You can see the myth present in everything.
If you stand back and look at the whole
With new eyes
You begin to see the patterns and relationships
Amongst and between all.
Over time and across distance,
The threads of a whole story become visible.
They merge into one picture
With infinite possibilities for change and movement.
A living sculpture,
Moving onward in time and place.

April 2013, Belfast

I see that the soul of Ulster
Is a bright golden colour now,
Beyond all of Orange and Green.
It is new, and it is what comes
When you empty a cauldron of hatred
And clean up the mess
So that people can stand up straight again.
This golden light is strong and beautiful.
And when you do see it,
It comes down from the hills
Like an aura of angels,
Full of love and peace and forgiveness.
Any who are in the path of it will weep.
These tears will leave the eyes shining,
Because the light of the soul
That comes through after such suffering
That the people of Ulster
Have had to endure,
Is a very healing light.
The light after suffering is different.
It is enduring,
Lasting.
The healed soul comes home
And there will be no more betrayals.

The last Friday in April finds me at a coaching conference in the Titanic Quarter, Belfast. In a departure from the norm, I am not delivering a presentation, workshop, meditation or any other form of energy work. Instead, I am attending a conference entitled *Back to The Future* and it is filling up with business leaders, coaches, executive coaches and managers from as far away as Dublin and Cork.[1] All are interested in the development of people and their performance within organisations, businesses and institutes of education and training.

But Brigid is here, too. And as we all file into the big assembly room for the opening address, I know that Brigid is here for a purpose, which, as yet, is not clear to me.

Niamh of the nut-brown hair has led the Association for Coaching in Ireland over the past five years and has successfully manifested a new vision. She welcomes us all, saying that she is delighted to have this conference in Belfast today. She introduces our first keynote speaker, Carole Pemberton, who talks about resilience.[2]

I met Carole in January 2012 at a meeting in the University of Ulster when a team gathered to design a new Masters course in coaching. After that meeting in Jordanstown, as I drove along the shore of Belfast Lough at dusk, I heard Brigid singing the *Soulsmith Song*. I knew then that she was asking me to pick up the threads of the work we did together in Belfast twelve years ago.

Although I have no idea how this conference today might be relevant to our mythic story, I trust that it will show itself before the day is out.

At lunchtime I gather in the eating area with my colleagues. A rapport is struck and the conversation is animated and focused. With the weather still quite raw for April, there are violent gusts of wind and rain rattling the windows beside us. I am cold in my sleeveless dress and I draw on my coat. Still listening to our conversation, I watch the ceaseless rivulets of water pour down the window and splash off the concrete onto the courtyard outside. I am wondering about Brigid and our myth.

Later, we gather again in the large assembly hall for the final keynote address – *Intelligent Organisations* – given by Brian Smyth.[3]

'Support people into the joy of their lives, so they can find and awaken the angels of beauty within,' he says.

'Listen to his words,' Brigid whispers.

I sense the power of his address opening the hearts and uplifting the spirits of the people sitting around me. Now I know why Brigid has called me here today. Brigid is the Goddess of poets and wordsmiths, healing and crafting, creativity and imagination. Ultimately, she is the Goddess of transformation.

Brian Smyth asks us to look for the natural intelligence in everything around us. Highlighting the importance of observing nature, learning from its cycles and taking that wisdom into the organisations in which we work.

'Men like him will support the return of feminine light,' Brigid comments, nodding with approval. She wants to see her light in all workplaces in Ulster so every person can be infused with the 'angels of beauty' within them.

Brian shows us an inspiring video of the musical conductor Leonard Bernstein[4], a leader who inspired superb ensemble performances from his orchestras.

Brigid nudges me. She reminds me that in my last year of school, at seventeen, I became the leader of the County Down Youth Orchestra. It was a year when inspiration came in from everywhere for me. I matured through the music and I learned how the confidence, mood and timbre of the lead violin's playing were crucial to the outcome for the concert performance.

All through my teenage years I played the violin, first in the County Antrim, and subsequently in the County Down, Youth Orchestras. Music kept a spark alive and fanned the flames that would give me a lifelong joy in playing the violin. A counterpoint of light to the darkness of the Troubles of the North in the 1970s.

By the age of eighteen I understood the balance of light and dark, played out in many pieces. I knew the nuances that make good music. There is a power in music to uplift and transform everything around us. The epiphany of its form. Its power to soften the heart and renew the spirit.

I understand fully what Brian Smyth is asking us to consider. It is for the conductor to bring out the beauty in each person's performance as set by the composer and allow each the joy to perform at his or her best. The orchestra has a parallel in business: He is calling us to be leaders within our organisations, with the imagination to create ensembles within the members of our teams that expand and allow into everything the magic of something beyond words.

Brigid asks: 'Can you remember what it was like to lead the orchestra?'

I recall an evening concert in 1976, in a secondary school in north Down. I stand up and signal with my bow to the lead oboe player, asking for a note to tune our instruments. The long note goes on and on until we are all in tune. It signals a quiet in the audience and we gather our energy to begin. The conductor raises his baton and with his downward strike the first players come in. At the beginning, we violins are waiting, counting eight bars of rest. It is Schubert's *Unfinished Symphony*. We come in gently with the fast notes of the *pianissimo*, and our whisper brings in the oboe and clarinet in their lovely, lyrical dance. All moving towards a crescendo and, exactly when he lifts the baton, we come to a sudden stop. Wait again ... and here is the cello solo playing the smooth refrain that will echo over and over again through the whole piece. We violins are in again with sudden jolts, shocks, changing the answer to the cello call and upping the power. Aah, now quiet ... and here again is the refrain. A deep, earthed sound from the double bass, like a lion awakening from its sleep.

Although magnificently composed, this piece is challenging for the whole orchestra. We strive to match its pathos and power. The syncopation that lulls you into rest. Then the force of *fortissimo* suddenly shifts you out, all senses alert again. You keep one ear on your own playing and the other on the rest of the orchestra. You know exactly when the horns come in, the cello and the woodwind. You cannot break your concentration for a moment. You are part of a finely tuned ensemble.

Glancing upwards from the music, you keep your eye on the conductor. Following his emphasis, loud then quiet, keeping exact time with his beat. All is held in the gestures and movements of his hands that are light and flowing like a bird. Each instrument is directed in on cue and given a chance to shine.

At the finish, we draw out the long notes of harmony to the triumphal final chord. In response to the conductor's uplifting arms, you get up on your feet, and then signal with your hand to the rest of the players. You turn towards the audience and, as the whole orchestra follows you to stand, all bow together to receive the applause.

Seeing the light in my eyes as I remember the joy of a concert performance, Brigid smiles at me. She continues: 'It is the rightful place for women to be leaders in this culture. Once Macha lifted her curse in 1999, she opened the pathways for healing. The gathering in Belfast in 2000 helped to call home the Ulster soul. In the years since then, the healing process has continued and the feminine is now strong in all walks of life. Women are becoming empowered again and taking their places as leaders within this culture. You are witnessing this today in the women who are running this conference, supported by the men here. The feminine can only reassert itself in the world when the masculine is sufficiently healed to allow them to do so.'

Reflecting on the theme of Schubert's *Symphony No. 8*, I think of the North of Ireland. The unfinished North. Brigid and Macha are working together to bring back the feminine into the heart of Ulster and help create a new culture. New words to find us. Angels of beauty everywhere. And, whereas Macha's healing is restoring the wildness in both women and the soul of the land, Brigid's transforming light moves in and through the cultures of people, should they allow her to do so.

As Brian finishes his talk, I sense light coming down from the Belfast Hills: Black Mountain, Divis and Cavehill. And, as this light steals its way across the city and enters into the room here, I can even hear angels singing. I know it is the light that I saw rising from Lough Neagh in February. Brigid's light.

As the talk ends, I jump up to clap. Tears of joy are pouring down my face. It is another piece of the jigsaw that I have been searching for. Two rivers have finally come together in me. The light from a spiritual journey is meeting the material world of education, business and organisational development.

I look at the people around me. Everyone is feeling the achievement of this day. In the centre aisle my colleagues are gathering. I join them to congratulate Niamh on the success of the day:

Oh, Niamh of the nut-brown hair,
Take us back to the future
And let the future come to us,
So we can release the past,
And step into the light of tomorrow.

The rest of my friends are heading back to Derry. I am going to visit my sister Margaret and her husband Brendan for a relaxing evening. Dinners with them are always enjoyable, with good conversation and nourishing food. Over the sixteen years since I moved to Donegal, I have spent many evenings at their home, always a place of warmth and welcome.

I don't ask for a lift to the train station. Instead, needing fresh air and space, I leave the building alone and take myself out into the squall and rain. In gusty winds and intermittent showers, I walk along the empty roadways of the Titanic Quarter towards the city centre. I climb up some steps onto a white footbridge and stop to lean over the railings and look beneath me at the turbulent waters of the Lagan. An eclipsed full moon last night has the sea rolling into Belfast Lough with its spring-tide power pushing against the flow of the river. The river itself is full to the brim with the endless heavy rain of recent weeks.

I stop and watch for a time. A large wave, rolling brown and dense, draws me into a trance. This place where I stand, looking down at the cream surf on these waves, becomes the bridge of two worlds. It is a place where past and present are opening to the future. Uniting all opposites: female and male, spirit and matter, moon and sun. In this altered place of poised stillness, I can see the turbulent roll of this water washing away all the differences in this culture, cleansing and dissolving the memories of pain, trouble and loss. Making 'new' so all might live.

Leaving the footbridge, I cross the road into the busy city centre streets. The rain has stopped and I am walking quickly up High Street to reach Great Victoria Street railway station. Passing a gift shop full of green gimmicks, Aran jumpers and things faux-Irish, I hear the music of *The Galway Girl* blasting out to the street, with Sharon Shannon on her accordion, playing out the chorus with her mighty power.[5] It is one of the tunes we play in our music sessions in Greencastle.

Singing out loud and dancing my way up through the city centre in my elegant conference clothes, I am fourteen again. I remember clearly the girl I was then.

In the early 1970s, the whole culture was crushed and fragmented, harsh and dangerous. We had moved into a cauldron of darkness in the North of Ireland; so complex, so deep, how could anyone get to the bottom of it? It exploded outwards and made shards of people's lives as they scrambled to hold onto something of common decency. There was little chance of a teenage girl being connected with the Goddess. Rather than blossom, the young feminine was starved.

We are a generation of people, now in our fifties, who were teenagers in the '70s. Vulnerable as we were, maturing into young women and men, we survived within the darkness of the North in a myriad of different ways. I went to discos where fights broke out and I saw teenage girls tearing chunks of hair from other girls' heads and kicking them to the floor. The legacy of Macha's power in her wounded and cursing place lived within us all. The culture was full of rage.

And today, with Macha's healed life force in every cell of my body, I am my fourteen-year-self dancing along High Street, reclaiming the joy that was missing in Belfast in those dark times. It is never too late to heal the fragmented soul.

Brigid speaks to that girl in me: 'There's a whole new world waiting to be born. Release and shed, hold your head up, Daughter. Let go of the shame. Let go of the grief. I will not let go of your hand. Walk with us now towards the light and help to create the new tomorrow.'

I continue to dance and sing up through the streets of Belfast, delighted that in 2013, no-one takes any notice of me. I start running to avoid the rain and, reaching the station, rush through with ticket in hand to jump on board a waiting train, singing the words of a Percy French song:

Are ye right there, Michael, are ye right?
Do you think that we'll be there before the night?
Ye've been so long in startin'
That ye couldn't say for certain
Still ye might now, Michael,
So ye might![6]

CHAPTER ELEVEN
Forgiveness

Ulster is a special place.
The people are full of passion and wit,
Sharpness and honesty.
The soul is deep and deeply damaged.
It is a flow of goodwill from all of us that creates healing.
You simply do what is asked for, trust and keep going.
Later, you might see signs that tell you
That, indeed, something has shifted.
With Macha's curse dissolved,
What would the Healed Feminine look like?
What will bring kindness back into the heart of Ulster?

May 2013, Moville

The power to forgive comes slowly through.
We reach it
In a quiet place of highest soul
And deepest silence.
In the moment
'We are sorry'
Is said,
The dark anger
And shame is lifted off
Centuries of pain.
When the rage is transformed
From the soul and we can all say:
'I release you of the wrongs you did,
I let you go',
Kindness is brought back
Into the heart of Ulster.
The vicissitudes through time
Are healed by the light
Of true forgiveness.

A week after the conference in Belfast, I decide to take a break from writing and paint my house in Moville. I listen to music as I work. The days flow by. The walls are clean and new. Stone white.

After a week of this, Laura, a close friend from Ohio, and her daughter Yarrow arrive for a visit. They help put the sitting room back in order and we go out to a music session in Greencastle.

The following morning we sign up for a tour of the Walls of Derry.[1] Walking along the streets of the city, we hear the stories of its history. We look over the Walls to the Bogside at the mural of a young girl shot dead in 1971 aged just fourteen.[2] As I listen to these stories I weep tears in the rain, walking along with this group of tourists holding colourful umbrellas. I was thirteen in 1971. Releasing. Releasing.

The following week I paint my hall. I listen to country fiddle music and think about all the people I have known in Derry since the 1980s who have contributed to the building of peace: community workers, teachers, youth leaders, musicians, lecturers, workshop facilitators, dramatists and artists. In recent years, the crystal healers have brought in a subtle energy as they built on all that went before, gathering the thin threads of light already woven in those dark days of the '80s and '90s.

One of the energy healers will join me on Saturday for a celebration of Bealtaine. As I prepare the upstairs room, now empty of everything and perfect for a day's retreat, I look out the window at the brown furrows of the field ploughed ready for its summer crop. It will be a day to celebrate Danu, Mother Goddess of abundance.

On Sunday morning I drive into Derry, to the University of Ulster at Magee. I am going to join the delegates who have been attending a conference on peace building. It is timely, given my musings all week, and I sign up for a session in healing theatre.

Over lunch I engage in conversation with a group of young people from the US. I take the time to speak with the conference organisers who now have several programmes running in the study of International Peace Building using creative methods to release trauma, heal memory and move forward with life.[3] I take stock of the many years since the 1980s when the city was buzzing with a wealth of creative arts, all of which paved the way for new beginnings.

On Monday, the last week in May, I begin to paint the final room upstairs. I am filled with a great uplift of spirit after the two events, the Danu retreat and the peace conference. As I climb up the step ladder to reach into the corners, enjoying the warmth of the sunlight coming into the room,

I am in the future, years ahead. I paint a bright new story into these walls and, as I do, I see the power of mythology pouring in to support the people who are creating change. Carrying the fruits of everyone's work here into a bright new future. The light of peace that is joining hearts and uplifting minds everywhere. I am singing.

A week later, I have finished and am in my sitting room, filled now with beauty. Macha has come into the room and I get the scent of summer flowers as she settles down in the sofa and looks at the newly painted white walls.

She asks me: 'After this year, Brigid's light and mine are now joined and the light of women is returning to the land and soul of Ulster. Do you think people will open their hearts and let beauty and joy come into everyday life?'

I pause and look out the window at the lavender bushes in my garden and the green lawns beyond. And beyond that again I can see the water of Lough Foyle.

I turn back and look at her, aware of a settled peace in me now, and I say: 'The simplicity of everyday things imbued with meaning creates an ambience that nurtures the soul. Is it not in these pleasures of life in communion with others, for a moment or a lifetime, that allows in the light of a new tomorrow while you simply sit and sip the sweetness of today?

'This kind of soul energy is a flow of both alike and different. It blends, respects and loves what is in all of its diversity. It seeks not to divide but to unify and find simplicity. A tolerance that can come to all of us in this land of differing religions, cultures and genders. It is a light that points the way to a new tomorrow.'

My words flow out of the window and are wafting around the lavender. A pause, a breath. The orange marigold smiles at me as I let the words go.

When I look back at Macha, still on the sofa, she is regarding me with a soft smile: 'Your words are eloquent today, Daughter, echoing the shimmer off these walls. Tell me, in the light of all these subtle shifts around you, what would lifting the curse mean to you now?'

I take a deep breath and, returning her smile, reply: 'I want to say to people: Look with new eyes and find the human, tender, grieving, fragile, beautiful, sparkling, weeping, laughing eyes that you see in every person you meet. Use not your eyes to curse one another, but use your eyes to bring in kindness and softness, blessing and love.

'I want to say: The war is gone. The curse is lifted. Who are we now and who do we want to be?'

A quiet Sunday morning. I have moved the meditations from Tirrion to my newly painted house in Moville. This morning we will do *Spirit of the Wind*.[4] Deep peace.

A cool cleansing breeze. A white curtain blows in the open window. Sitting here are six women who have come from Tyrone, Inishowen and Belfast. Here in this room we have business women, lecturers, shamanic practitioners and healers. When each woman came into the room, a flow of seasoned, mature female energy entered with them. All sit, quietly waiting for the session to begin.

Present here is another woman I knew in primary school. I see in her twinkling brown eyes and cheeky smile the girl that she was then. All the years between us, from girls to women, melt as we begin our meditation and quietly enter the silence.

'Breathe in to deepen and relax. Breathe out to release. Hold in stillness. Be aware of all in your life about which you are seeking clarity ...' I hear my voice speaking, slowing down, connecting.

I hear Macha's voice softly behind me: 'Gather now, women of Ulster, in circles of power and respect for each other. Let the spirits of the elements assist you to find your places of leadership in a brightly forming new world. Look for the deeper soul within the worlds of commerce and trade.'

I look around at the women gathered with me. Faces in quiet contemplation. As we finish and come slowly out of the silence, few words are spoken. A small fire lit earlier in the grate has gone out. Wind is stronger today than fire. We move to the kitchen for tea.

A few days later, I am out at the little house at Tirrion recalling winter nights here of deep peace. The sounds of the waterfall in the valley can no longer be heard at night, muffled now by the foliage of the trees.

I rise at dawn and sit outside in an armchair listening to the early morning bird song. At intervals, the cuckoo's echo comes back and forth. Growth is returning to the land. The soaring of spirit and joy is in everything. Thinking of gardens and flowers and beauty and growth, I wonder what might be left here for the ancestors, to thank them for the healing that has been given.

I ask the spirits in the valley: 'What shall I plant in the garden here at the little house in memory of this time?'

They whisper back: 'For the Grandmothers of the land at Tirrion, plant roses, wild and strong. Ones with rich colour and fragrant bloom.'

In June 2013, I plant out the back garden of my house in Moville. I dedicate it to Grandmother Katie and her family, those kinfolk of mine who have long since departed. I never walked in her garden as she died before I was born.

With gratitude for everything, I plant a river of strength and colour. Honeysuckle, rock rose, marigolds and sweet William. I plant a pale peach rose especially for her.

In the centre I plant a flower bed for my brother John, with the pink mallow called lavatera, surrounded with purple lupin, white columbine and bright yellow lilies. Perennials, whose blooms are dancing today in the sunlight on this lovely afternoon. The soft sound of angels singing fills my heart with joy.

A month later, as its pink flowers begin to emerge, the green leaves of the lavatera weep tears in the morning dew.

PART IV
Rebirth

CHAPTER TWELVE
Malinbeg

Ceaseless sound
Of water in a cove
Wind on the skin
Sun is warming
Smell of the sea
Cry of seagulls
Elements eternal
The earth is strong
Rock crystals
A renewal of spirit

June 2013, Malinbeg

I am at the Silver Strand beach, Malinbeg, on the southwest coast of Donegal. I spend some time sitting quietly on a rock by the waterfall at the far end of the beach. I hold my hands in pools of its sparkling essence, its cool freshness cleansing me as I recall the events of the past six years.

My spirit was called to Tirrion, to put roots there and build a house. But what transpired was completely different. Not a solid built house at all but another whole mythic story with Macha and healing in Ulster. The ancestors of the land there in the glen calling me and connecting me with Grandmother Katie. It is a year since we did the healing with her and the Rose Quartz.

As I sit here today and let this water flow over my hands, I can see my gardens at Moville and Tirrion with the flowers I planted for everyone. In my picture, a river of rain is flowing through all of it, washing it down. Deep release. The old patterns are going now and light is coming in, bringing forgiveness, beauty and joy.

I sense a presence in the middle of the strand and when I look over I see Macha walking in the shallow waters of puddles left on the sand as the tide went out. I see her bend down to pick up shells. As I walk towards her she looks up, sees me and smiles. I smile at the quiet entrance she has made onto this beach today. Macha is at home here in the elemental wildness. Intense, raw and achingly beautiful. Her head is circled with a crown of fired gold from the mountains. Her aura shines brightly around her, like a cloak of sparkling silver, and matches the dance of light on the surface of the sea. Her hair is damp in the soft rain that is blowing in the wind. This wind has come from the west. It is filled with the memories of the waves and the ocean. It smells of freedom.

As the distance between us closes, I feel the weight of

the months and years fall away from me. I sigh a deep breath and run towards her, power seeping into me from the very sand itself. As I approach her she straightens up and, still holding the shells, opens her arms to welcome me. Her holding is of ages. In the warmth and strength of her embrace, I weep.

Macha is saying something to me, although her lips do not move: 'When I called you north all those years ago, I did not know how long it might be. A healed and tender heart is what you are left with. Let joy flow in like water to your whole being and allow it to come into everything you do.'

As I look out at the sea, calm today in summer sunshine, I reflect on all the years since I came north in December 1996 in answer to Macha's call: *Return, Daughter, return.*

Macha is fingering each shell carefully and shows me those in her hand: 'The shells collected here in the ebb and flow of tides all tell a story of each piece of the journey. Gathering the memories of everything. All those years since you came to this beach in a bleak January of 1997 to gather the quartz stones for the Brigid workshop in Glencolmcille. The years since we saw the oranges on the beach in 1999. The Star Captain – he was a part of those years of fertile work in Donegal. His friendship anchored you in the journey you made with the land. He was a part of the wider myth. A beloved. Your spirits were matched and deeply connected.'

She looks out at the sea and her hair blows wild. I look upwards at the seagulls above us. Seagulls and their babies, flying over and back in the gentle breeze that is here today. I remember the times walking on the beach with the Star Captain. I truly loved him. A prince of the Dananns.

'I never knew if it was real or not, that relationship with him,' I say to Macha. She turns to me and smiles.

'It was real within the otherworldly spaces you occupied. Within the ordinary world it was mercurial, never quite manifesting into anything of substance that you could hold onto. You and he were together in the myth and your spirits were lent to each other until that work was done.'

She has that faraway look again and turns her head to look towards the sea. Her words flow out into the soft air: 'We are all in a story and sometimes the story is bigger than we are. Take my story with Cruinniuc. Who knows what it might have been, or could have been, if he had not boasted of me to the King?'

Macha continues: 'You came back into the northern energy fields in 2007, but not in the way you thought, nor to do the work you imagined. But it was done anyway. It was about the healing of men. It was the music that helped to heal the men of Ulster. Every time you played with your group of lovely Ulstermen, energy was sent out on chords of colour. Spreading across the land, it helped to heal the collective soul of men. Music calls forth the courage for men to be vulnerable. And the acceptance of their vulnerability helps men to express emotions in ways that will not destroy the women around them. The wives and daughters of all the men who were touched by that music will feel the benefit for many years to come. In this realm and in other realms, it all reached its mark.'

A chill comes into the air and a wave of wind goes by us. I pause to take in all of what she is saying. I finally understand it. The intelligence behind the myth. The way everything is connected and in this wider picture it all has meaning.

Macha continues: 'Before you close this story, go back and ride horses again. Sit in the raw truth of everything.'

As she speaks, I see a vision opening before me.

'The raw truth is the old, old woman in the woods who will not be seen for fear of surrender. Raw, like a witch in a forest at night-time, sitting on an old block of wood under a moonlit sky. She is shuffling her feet back and forth in the piles of dead leaves on the ground as she mutters a chant. Her feet start to move in a wild rhythm to this beat. Her hair, long and strangled around her head, is matted with cow dung. She is spitting into the fire, cursing the ages of man that have put her here in this dark forest.'

Macha continues: 'Find the horses in Moville and sit with all of this. They have called you now, ride with them again. The horses will take you back to the Grandmothers in Sligo and the ancient places of this land where the guardian spirits await the telling of your story.'

A spread of golden soul across Ulster.
Songs in the wind.
Beloved returns to me as I to him.
A warrior takes a rest.
A woman, whole,
Dances on a beach,
Feet wet and cold
From sand and salt water.
Watches a flock of seagulls above her,
Their wings spreading to soar,
In harmony with her dance.
Life is rich
When all things are in place.

CHAPTER THIRTEEN
Soul of the Horse

Awakening to the horse soul
Means awakening to a spark of life.
The dawn of new.
Emotional, physical and mental skills,
Flow together in this pursuit.
All of them needed
To ride a horse with competence.

July 2013, Moville

A bright summer evening. The white walls of my house in Moville glow with light. The beauty here carries a welcome for all.

Dressed in light cotton tops and colourful summer skirts and trousers, five women arrive at the door bringing food. These are my coaching colleagues from Derry. We are here this evening to celebrate our year together. Connected to each other in a spirit of collective learning, we gather to do a meditation with the *Spirit of Water*.[1]

I bring my reflections from the waterfall at Malinbeg to this gathering now and hold the intention to ask this element to wash us clean: 'Breathe in. Breathe out. Bring your whole attention into this moment. Visualise a waterfall of cleansing around you. See it flowing through your aura. Let it wash away what no longer serves. Release and let in the light of the new. Come home to your own centre. Come home to yourself.'

After our meal, we drive to the path along the shore of Lough Foyle for a walk in summer sunshine. My cousin Margaret, one of our coaching colleagues, steps out at a fast pace. I join with her, leaving the rest of the group strolling behind us.

As I look down at our feet moving swiftly across the path, we are matching stride for stride. A physical mirror for each other. Our mothers were sisters and we carry in our bones a deep kinship from that north Antrim female line. Reared on fresh sea air, we spent childhood summers on beaches of sand and sunshine. Her mother is still alive and living in Derry. Without missing a beat, she and I keep pushing forward along the shore.

A week later, I am standing at my front door in Moville and looking out over Lough Foyle. I sense the presence of horse spirits with me at the doorstep. Cooley Equestrian

Centre is over the hill. Their horse trails are visible from my garden. I go to meet Gillian, the woman who runs the stables, and arrange a date for my first lesson.

It is most interesting that in a shamanic practice you can talk easily to the spirit of horses and never be afraid of them. As soon as you climb on the back of a real horse, a primitive fear kicks in. It becomes a matter of survival. Riding a horse can be dangerous and you need to take great care. Being strong in body and mind is essential. This reality mocks all of the connection you think you have with the spirits of animals.

However, what you slowly realise is that the horse or pony you are riding will meet you where you need to be met. It will take care of you if you can learn to ask, trust and be with it. The horses of this herd at Cooley are a special team as they are trained and fostered to support therapeutic riding.[2] Their spirits are finely tuned to the needs of their riders. They have called me to ride with them and I will learn over a whole summer to trust what this means in relation to my story with Macha.

A few weeks on and, with one lesson behind me, I am leading Peanuts out of the stable this morning for my first trek along the lanes at Cooley. He is a feisty pony with a dark-brown coat and a wiry black mane. Light on his feet, he dances along the path down to the arena. A cheeky boy, hungry for greens, he grabs at the leaves of the hedge. I pull him away and yet I am hesitant to exert my will. *Is he laughing at me?* This push and pull is a testing of wills. *Should I be in charge or is he?*

There are four of us on horses ambling out of the yard today. As we make the turn onto the road, a painful memory returns. Nine years ago I suffered a fractured collar bone from another small pony while holding him and waiting to ride.

Shocked with the sudden image of it, I freeze with fear. But wait! A strange calm comes over me and I am able to hear these words, spoken by the horse spirits: 'You are safe here. This cheeky pony will tease and test, but if you can trust him, he will help you to release the fear.'

I breathe deeply, relax and silently give my thanks. I gather my reins with renewed confidence and I sense, too, an ease in Peanuts. His spirit has come to meet the frightened girl in me.

On this fresh morning, bit by bit, within all of the ordinary things of riding out with four women – walking, trotting and chatting along roads and country lanes – I release the fear within me. Well able now to pull Peanuts away from the hedges, this ride today is profoundly healing.

A week after the hack with Peanuts, I am indoors and riding Star. She is a black mare cob with a small white blaze on her face. Her pace is measured and steady. Her back feels safe and solid. There are two of us having a lesson today. We steer our horses in ever-decreasing circles across the white lines of several poles that are laid in a careful pattern on the ground. These exercises are challenging, as they always are with Gillian's tuition. Each angle is different and awkward turns are necessary.

'Look where you are going in advance. By the time you are over the pole it is too late to make your turn.' Her voice is strong and directive, encouraging and supportive.

We have a lot of laughter and, in the ease between us all, I begin to feel a part of something bigger than just myself and my horse. I count five females in the space: two riders, two mares, and one teacher.

I sense a complete harmony of pace and rhythm as the whole arena vibrates with one connected flow of movement. As all merge to become a part of the herd, I experience 'entrainment', the intelligence of a group mind at work.

Back in the stable after the lesson, I enjoy the time to brush down my horse. I stroke Star's back in gratitude for her magic. How is she able to pace herself in such harmony with the rider? I ponder this gift in all of the horses here.

'I think I am making progress,' I say to Gillian.

'In your case,' she replies, 'it's not so much progress as an awakening. I think you were quite a competent rider all those years ago before you quit. And now it is simply helping your body to remember it again.'

Her intelligent eyes are smiling back at me. I look at her as she turns to go, greatly appreciating how sensitively she works with both the horses and the riders. She is lean and fit, light in mind and body. Her long hair is tied back in a ponytail under a peaked cap. Layers of clothes to keep warm. She listens deeply and makes clear decisions as to what is needed at any given time. The gift of her teaching is helping me to remember my skills in ever-increasing circles of confidence.

There is a rare heat in Donegal this summer and along with this is a peace in the air that is uplifting. I try to go riding every week. Mostly we are outdoors and today I am on Peanuts again.

I was asked to take up the rear of the ride and keep an eye on a young girl beside me. She is about eleven years old and riding a sturdy black pony called Annie. The two of us follow the four women on horses. All six creating a unison of rhythm. Two by two, ambling up the road. Enjoying my extra responsibility, I ride today with the easy grace of a seasoned horsewoman. The young girl beside me is well able to keep up with the women. Peanuts saunters along, very protective of the rear of all.

On our return, the yard is full of girls and a few young boys, all chatting excitedly to each other. There is a buzz of activity as all are preparing for a show tomorrow. They are cleaning, sponging and washing their horses. Some are decorating their horses' manes with ribbons and plaits.

I watch their faces and listen to their chat as they work. As the horses are led round in a circle to dry off, they shake their heads and swish their tails with delight. The clip-clop of their hooves is like music on the concrete yard. A female-grounded community, reflected in the faces of all. Horses and humans together. Harmonious beauty.

CHAPTER FOURTEEN
Wisdom of Mares

The voice of the horses
Speaks into the fabric of our souls
As the myth is mended and created anew.

July 2013, Moville

Last night I dreamt that Joanne, my horse from Sligo, was still alive and fit and able to take a rider on her back. In the dream, my mouth opens wide as I hear this news. A big smile lights up my whole being. I am in awe of the miracles that life can bring. My joy is immense. After all these years, I cannot believe that she is still here and I can simply walk over to her in the stable in Sligo, get up on her back and ride out again across the sand with the wind in my hair.

As I wake and realise it is a dream, I am aware of the disappointment as reality dawns. Aah ... so many circles, so much loss, so much change. And yet in the midst of it all, there are eternal moments where nothing is lost and the light of the heart remains forever.

I bend forward on Holly's back, put my face into her mane and drink in the deep mare magic of her. Holly is a beautiful horse. Large in height, with a dark-brown and black coat, she is sensual, like velvet. In the grace of her whole being there is a deep feminine silence. Holly meets me in the same place that Joanne met me all those years ago. It is a place within the womb, of felt 'womanness', deepening into the very earth herself.

As we ride out today along the roads, I take my ease to look upon the land around us. The silvery-grey, shimmering surface of Lough Foyle is below us and green hills roll out in the distance beyond. Very safe at this steady pace and held within this group of riders, I wonder how on earth I was able to ride Joanne alone, out across the strand in Sligo Bay, all those years ago?

I return to Moville after a long drive home, urgent to get to the stables before 6.00pm. It is bright and sunny with some sudden showers to freshen us.

Five of us leave the yard this evening. On Holly's back, my body moves fluidly with the steady gait of her walk. I enjoy being with these mature horsewomen. Sometimes I listen as they talk. Other times, I just breathe and quietly stay in the place that is Holly and I.

As we are walking up the road, there is a different feel to the air this evening. I sense something strange and new. A mysterious calm. Otherworldly almost. The sun is shining brightly but it is unsettled. The horses in the field are whinnying to us as we pass. Our horses call back to them, lifting their heads and shaking their manes. They quicken their walk.

Further down the road, a sudden shower of rain hits us. A rainbow spreads an arc of bright colours across the darkening sky. I sense the horses' edginess with this shifting energy around us, yet they are taking us riders into a strange communication with all of nature. They are moving us into a bigger story. It is as if we are riding out across the plains and hills and all five of us have been on this journey together many times, in many lifetimes.

Around the next corner, Gillian shouts: 'Open seat!' and lifts her hand. At her command, the five horses take off at speed up the lane. In a heartbeat, I lean easily into the rhythm of Holly's canter, settling into her strong and pulsing flow.

Back at the stables I am exhilarated. This has been a magnificent evening and my first time on the 'canter lane'. I realise that horses can bring you into a place of pure heart. The love they give in their relationship is one that brings joy and beauty to your whole sense of yourself.

It is a Thursday morning at the end of August. I am late arriving for the 10.00am start. I come into the arena and see ten riders and horses lined up, ready to go outside for the morning's trek. They include many of the young folk whom I saw in the yard a month ago preparing for the show. With them are Gillian and three older women. I see Peanuts waiting for me.

The morning air is dry and chilly with a touch of autumn.

I have not ridden with the young ones before and their excitement is tangible in the air. A wildness and carefree abandon as the summer holidays are coming to an end. As we ride out, I am struck by the elegance of these young riders. Although eager to push ahead of us older ones, they respectfully hold back their mares and ponies that are dancing with this same wave of magic that is running through us all. Negotiating every turn. Sometimes we are walking, sometimes trotting. Uphill, downhill.

We reach the lane almost an hour later and as we turn the last corner, in an instant, all ten horses are in a canter. In slow motion, I see a portal opening and a vision takes shape.

All of us have become queens, princesses and princes of the Tuatha Dé Danann. We are Macha's folk and in a mythic story with her. In this vision, we are no longer on the lane but galloping across the plains. The land of Cooley, once sacred in ancient times, is awakening with the drumbeat of the horses' hooves. Macha, herself on a horse, is leading us forward, pushing up the hills in a wild gallop.

It is the sound of Gillian's voice that brings me back into this reality. 'Overtake on the outside ...'

The images fade, the portal is closing. I am once again on the lane cantering with Peanuts. He is all-in-himself today and we are racing fast. As we move to the outside I do not think, I simply ride on and on, continuing to pass the horse in front. I hear the shouts behind as the young folk catch up. Breathless and cheering, all rein in at the top of the lane to trot and then walk. At the end of a magnificent summer, this is a moment to cherish.

A week later, I am on holiday in Ballycastle before the summer finally ends. The sea on the north Antrim coast is as cold as ice.

At Murlough Bay, my sister Colette and I plunge into the waves to swim. As we move through the water, the coldness is pulsing through our bodies. We emerge like twin goddesses, the ones they call Beauty and Joy. Reborn from the ocean. Sunlight flows through us and around everything here on this small, rocky beach. A day to cherish our ancestral grandmothers and the legacy they left us in our motherline: strong physical bodies, resilient spirits and a great love of the sea.

It is eleven years since our mother died. That was seven years after her visit to me on Inis Mór.

Truly a daughter of Macha, I sense my mother's wild spirit still with us: 'Thank you Mother, for the beauty and joy given in this land's eternal love for us.'

CHAPTER FIFTEEN
Winter

Horses don't speak in words
But their thoughts
Are conveyed in images
Across a line of connection with you.
Listen deeply,
Not with your ears
But with your whole being.
Then you will know
What they are telling you.
They always know
When you have heard them.
Their gestures will signal their response.
It is a language you can learn.

September 2013, Cooley

On a Monday morning I go to meet Gillian. I have asked her to speak on behalf of the horses and their innate intelligence. Beautifully connected to the equine soul, she has that gift of thinking like a horse.

In the sitting room of her house, as Gillian starts to tell stories of the many generations of mares and foals, colts and geldings that have passed through the stables here at Cooley, she moves into a different zone. A woman steeped in horse-lore all her life, she spins magic with her words.

'Horses are so willing to please. They are forgiving. They learn by association and at the beginning you try to make each experience a good one, a winning one, so that it imprints on their memory. It is their memories that guide them in good and bad experiences. It forms their view of the world and how they interpret any new challenge. Horses pick up people's emotions and moods instantly. They know what they are dealing with. They communicate and you learn over time what their gestures are saying to you. The horses know they are healing and helping with our clients who come here. In the herd it is female energy that is predominant. The alpha mare is in charge and all the horses know their place.'[1]

There is a pause. A light comes in and I sense a new presence. As Gillian is sharing these insights, gleaned over a lifetime of working with horses, it seems that the spirits of all of the horses over the years are coming into the room. They like what she is saying and they want to hear this conversation. What she holds is a deep knowledge of the equine species. Their physical, emotional, and spiritual intelligence. She carries this on from the generations of her family before her. She is one with them. A mare-woman among mares and horses. I sit in reverence with this quiet peace that has come in to join us.

As I reflect on the power of this presence, I wonder about the horses in Macha's story. Something was violated in the relationship between horses and the Horse Goddess and a powerful disharmony resulted. A betrayal so deep, I cannot find the words to say it. Macha and the horses were forced into a male way of being, their essence breached. And the horses know this. The soul of the horse carries this memory in its collective knowing. And our collective souls, women and horses, can heal the wrongs suffered by each.

The vibration of all of these thoughts resonates in the room, creating waves of energy and a healing light.

Macha likes this conversation. She is delighted to hear Gillian speaking about horse wisdom. 'It is a long time since I met with one who is able to work so sensitively with the spirit of horses and also has great practical and intuitive skills to guide the healing work with the people who come here,' she says.

She is pleased that I followed her guidance to find Gillian and chose to learn from her. 'This is as it should be,' Macha says, 'and, as yet, you are only beginning.'

After this day, Gillian and I embark together on a winter of intense learning. Sometimes I ride with the cheeky pony Peanuts and on other days I am mounted on the back of safe, strong Star. Learning the basics over and over, and gradually increasing my confidence and ability to ride, I am in a place of being nurtured in a trusting relationship with two ponies and a good teacher. Peanuts holds the little girl in me and teases and helps me to laugh. Star meets me in the teenage-girl place that is full of moods and insecurities, both hers and mine.

In the indoor arena I do many weeks of intense work: big circles, small circles, clockwise circles, anticlockwise circles. Open seat across the poles, bendy line around the coloured cones. Figures of eight, changing diagonals. Crossing the centre, changing the rein. Off the boards, on the boards.

Peanuts is always a joy to ride and I learn how to call his bluff when he is in a mood and playing games. We work easily together. He helps me to build steady rhythm, stamina and the power of buoyancy and forward drive.

'Ride from your core, relax your shoulders; straighten your spine, shoulders back. Stretch your legs through the heels, relax your knees, breathe.' Gillian is bringing in more and more detail. Encouraging, strengthening, building confidence. 'Keep the reins separate, don't cross your hands, keep a straight line from your shoulders and elbows. Use your hips to turn. Inside leg pushes out, outside leg guides the turn. Look ahead, let the horse know where you are going.'

Sessions with Star, herself an alpha-mare cob, require a deeper navigation of the moods between us. Through the winter I learn emotional congruency and the strength of my own leadership from her.

This is a morning to remember: Star is terrified of the sound of hail on the tin roof and is jumping to the side, spooked with every blast of wind she hears. I say out loud and hold firm with my body: 'You are safe, it is only hail and wind.'

She is listening to me and thus reassured, her body relaxes as she releases the fear. I have, in my encounters with her over these months, mastered some of my own fears and stepped up to take command of challenging moments.

When spring comes round and mornings are fine enough to go out, I ride again on Holly along the lanes and, with groups of others, on longer treks up along the bog roads close to the hills.

One afternoon I am out on a hack with three of the young women. These girls are very excitable today and my head is turned with their chattering. The horses and ponies are dancing skittish in response to this high energy. It makes me very nervous to be near them on a horse. However, as we kick into a canter at the bottom of the lane, I find the power of connection with Holly to hold her back a pace from the others, allowing me to relax. Holly knows exactly what I am asking her to do and I feel the pulse of energy that flows through both of us, as we become one in thought and action. Moving in a beautiful, smooth canter, we hold, in every sinew, a steady pace and balance.

I reach the top of the lane behind the others. I know the gift that Holly has given me. A moment of perfection.

One of the girls asks me as we catch our breath before heading out on the road: 'Did Holly canter for you at all?'

'Yes, she did,' I say, 'one of the best ever.'

The voice of the horses
Speaks into the fabric of our souls
As the myth is mended and created anew.

CHAPTER SIXTEEN
Grandmothers of the Mountains

I hear the majestic Grandmothers of this land
Singing to me,
Calling me home.
Their voices blend with the mountains,
Keelogyboy, Crockauns, Knocknarea,
Deerpark and Benbulben.

March 2014, Sligo

In the spring of 2014, after all these years, I go again to find the Grandmothers in Sligo. Two mythical swans guide me to a place of sanctuary in the region of Keelogyboy Mountain in County Sligo. A beautiful house belonging to a dear friend provides a base beside a lake and a forest for the next stage of the journey. I am to spend several months here finishing the book. The land here is deep and silent. A womb to hold all. On many days I sense the spirits of horses running in the fields.

I hear the majestic Grandmothers of this land singing to me, calling me home. I realise as I listen to their song that they are the higher intelligence that has been guiding this entire journey. These Grandmothers of 'past, present and future' shall take the story to its next stage and, as Macha and I join again in the landscape of Sligo where we first met twenty-two years ago, the Grandmothers shall help to weave the final threads of the journey from beginning to end.

One morning I am in the sunroom at the front of the house speaking with Macha. As we sit, the branches of trees in the forest beyond us become like fingers in the wind, swaying and moving. Hypnotic in their rhythm, they open up pictures of a world beyond this one.

There is a thundering of horses' hooves as we speak and the ground is shaking and shifting. I look out of the window and see a vision of people on horses coming out of the woods. Each horse glides into a clearing of grass and circles around. The horses stand motionless. I lean closer to see what is happening. There are about twelve young women and four older women.

'They are the children of the Silver Branch,' Macha explains, 'young women riding out with the Dé Danann queens and goddesses, learning to weave the dreams of the people into patterned forms of energy. Sharpening their senses to timing and meeting, to contrast and speed. Watch them and see ...'

As the circle is formed, the horses bow their heads and the women respond with a bow of their heads across to each other. All now hold a stillness in their being. It is a unified cameo, choreographed into place. They are dressed in rich, bright colours. A Queen on a white horse has a dark-green and gold cloak. Another Queen, attired in reds and browns, is sitting on a chestnut mare. A third mature and stately woman is in robes of silver, turquoise and royal blue and she is perched proudly on a silver dappled pony.

'She is a Goddess from Munster province,' Macha whispers.

Four of the young women are attired in red and gold with sparkling jewels. They are mounted on horses of different colours: a pale dun, a chestnut, a dark-brown bay and a silver white. Another four are dressed in turquoise like the sea, with silver shimmering. All of these four are on dappled grey horses of various shades from silver to beige. Four other young girls are in the colours of nature, wearing dresses of rust and brown and bright green; one with auburn hair glistening in the sun. Another's fair hair is plaited into a wreath of green rushes and spring flowers. She is wearing a gown of pale green silk. Next to her is a small dark-haired girl in a cream dress of simple linen. White flowers are pinned onto her hair; it shines like the ebony of her horse. Their faces are alive and vital, filled with light.

Starting to move again, they all turn alternately right then left and, in an instant, have skipped forward into a trot round the circle. The horses begin to peel off in different directions weaving over and back on lines across the circle.

Four groups have now formed and are coming to meet each other from different directions. Crossing at the centre line of the circle, they weave in and out in precise timing. Figures of eights, I can see as they move. In and around each other, patterns forming and changing. Now, spirals are taking shape.

Macha says: 'Horses enjoy this dance and movement. They feel the patterns in their bodies and resonate with the harmony and precise timing of it. Their herd nature allows for good teamwork and they nourish one another with the energy. Horses enjoy the nobility of racing. They like the beauty of this.'

I sit in silence and watch as the horses and riders come to a standstill, bow again to each other and begin to stream out of the clearing back into the forest. It is a sight to behold and never to be forgotten.[1]

'Horses and Horse Daughters,' Macha repeats a line she often says. I can see that we have moved into the realm of the Tuatha Dé Danann. The triple Goddess of 'mother, maiden and crone' is coming to support the blossoming of the young feminine. Teaching women the power of creating new forms as they partner with the wisdom of the horses.

After what seems ages, Macha has gone and I am aware of the presence of an ancient force beside me. This is a power that reaches back in time, far beyond Macha's story. This power is like the mountains, the old women and ancestors all combined in one voice. Larger than life, protective, maternal. The rivers of time are flowing through it. Rich with the colours of soul and love, it is held in the rivers and the mountains by the singing voices of old Grandmothers. It seems to be the higher intelligence behind the whole unfolding of the universe.

I remember the time when I first became aware of it. It was in the late 1980s when I was creating outdoor theatre performances from the mythical stories of the Tuatha Dé

Danann in Sligo. This ancient creative, female force has been with me since that time.

Several months later, I am out early one morning at Strandhill beach in Sligo. A vast expanse of flat, firm sand surrounds me. There is no-one around and no other sound but the waves gently lapping. I finish a round of T'ai Chi and stay watching the waves.

A soft misty autumn morning, I have just returned from a week in Kerry and it seems that the strange half-light enveloping this beach today has travelled from there and is bathing the whole west coast of Ireland in its magical, Munster glow. The mountains, Knockalongy to the south and Benbulben to the north, are not visible today in the haze. Time is standing still and I am aware of the presence of the spirits here. As I breathe, I merge with the waves. In this altered state a vision opens up.

I hear the drumbeat of hooves on the strand. I turn round and see in the distance a woman on a bright cream-coloured horse approaching me at a steady canter. The beauty and power of their union is breathtaking to watch. As she comes closer, she and the horse start to circle round. She reins in the mare, slips off its back and runs towards me. She is of medium height, wearing a red sweater and moss-green jeans. Her light brown hair is tousled with damp mist. As she runs, her face is aflame with light. I open my arms to greet her and the tears are streaming down my face. The horse is Joanne and this woman is myself at thirty-three years.

Holding her in my arms, I stroke her hair and wipe the tears from her cheeks. Joanne follows the young woman over to me. She paws at the ground and whinnies. This horse that gave me so much healing as a younger woman nuzzles her head against me, softly snorting warm breath. She has kept the wild, confident, younger me so safe for over twenty years. In bringing the power of this young woman back to me, Joanne's job is done and she throws back her head, kicks her heels and gallops off into the distance. I catch a glimpse of her coat and her bright cream mane flying out behind her as she disappears into the mist. And, as circles of many lifetimes come round again, worlds within worlds can meet. You can reach out and put your finger on the place where it all started.

The distance of years falls away and everything between 1990 and now in October 2014 dissolves into the air of this quiet morning. Forgiven and washed clean in new waters, everything innocent and untested that was within me then is within me again. Restored and whole. I stay a long time in the embrace with the younger-woman-me until I am aware of only the quiet swish of the waves and I am alone again on the beach.

The vision has passed. There is a crow squawking in the sky above me. As I walk to the car park, the crow continues her loud rant all the way back along the strand. I know she is a spirit sign of Macha's presence, witnessing the vision that just occurred. She flies off and I turn again for one last look at the waves.

In the winter of 2014, I go back to Moville each weekend. After my encounter with the spirit of Joanne on the strand in Sligo, my riding deepens significantly. There is no gap now between the physicality of riding Holly and the ongoing connection of being with Holly's spirit. It is as though I opened to a universe of horses' souls. I feel it in every nerve and sinew: *They have let me in.*

On a sparkling November morning, with the crisp air

of early winter, Gillian and I are on a hack, riding gently around the lanes at Cooley. From our vantage point high on the hills we can see the waters of Lough Foyle shimmering beneath us.

There is a strong magical energy off the lough today. Something new is breaking through on this fine Samhain morning. All the countryside around Cooley is vibrating with us, calling the ancient ones of this sacred place in Inishowen to sing again as the power of Macha's story continues to spread out across the land.[2]

CHAPTER SEVENTEEN
The Silence Before Birth

Go back to the hills where it all began
And offer your story to them.
In a place of deep peace,
Under the mountains,
Close to the lake
And within a sanctuary surrounded by trees,
Still your body,
Breathe and just be.
Go down into the silence of the land.

October 2014, Emain Macha

The hills are quiet and the air is still. Occasionally there is the sound of a bird singing. Go even deeper into the silence until you come to the very centre of the land. It is a place of mystical grey-green light and here you will find the magical truth of ancient Ireland. Breathe it in, fill your lungs with this otherworldly air. Taste and savour it. Take it into your bones.

This is the liminal place where Irish myth reshapes itself anew for the story of tomorrow. A mythical place linked with the sacred hills of Uisneach and Emain Macha. The Grandmothers of 'past, present and future' are calling in the power of the mountains across the land. The mountains are those majestic beings that brought their healing power to this story over years and years. As they hear this note sounding out across the land, Slieve League, the hills in Glenties, the Belfast Hills, Emain Macha and all of the mountains in County Sligo are reverberating now with one unified voice.

Rainbows of colour bring in the light of healing from the waters in the lakes, waterfalls, streams and rivers. Lough Neagh, Lough Foyle, the Lagan, the Owenea, the Unshin and the little streams all over the northern counties. Their waters flow through all, cleansing and releasing. Ancestors are streaming in on these rivers of song that move across the land. Horses gallop in to be here in this wondrous place. The horses of the Tuatha Dé Danann, Margit's horses from Ardun House, and the herd at Cooley are all coming to witness this today.

From the stars and the moon, the sun and the sky and from the deepest oceans, the seedbeds of life are gathering here in this mythical place. Sit with us all and listen to the ending of this tale.

All life around is motionless in the pregnant pause that

is waiting for the new about to be born. The horses have stopped in their tracks. The swans are poised like statues at the side of the lake. You can see the young queens and princes of the Tuatha Dé Danann sitting on their horses, proudly waiting. The gallop of other horses is thundering on the earth over miles and miles of journey.

You can hear the endless prayer of the old women who sit in forests over fires, lit to ease the long nights. Old women have been waiting for a spark to hit the soul of men. Waiting for the Kings and fathers and mortal men to bow down and release their unholy hold on women's bodies and souls. Waiting for the land and the mountains to spew up the poisons dumped onto them by human weakness. Waiting for the lakes and wells and rivers that have held the tears of women, men and children to be emptied of grief and refilled with the sparkling, fresh hope of a new dawn.

Old women are waiting for all of this as they spit their chewed-up rage and impotence into the fires. Sitting on soft beds of moss, with the fresh scent of pine in their forests, they are waiting for that moment when the air will change and leaves will rustle on the trees and all might be made new again. Power will be taken back by those who have been crushed and broken by distortions of truth and life and nature.

The trees in this magical place sway in the wind and join with the song of the trees in all the forests of Donegal and the northern counties as they release the burdens of what they have carried for us.

The Grandmothers of the mountains are singing a cradle song. Over and over, they gently chant the melody, welcoming the ragged old women as they emerge from the forest. 'Yes, old women, your time has come. Leave your fires in the forests and walk out into the light of day.'

All around start to move. Back and forth comes a wave of slow swaying. Building up. Spreading out. Soothing all.

As the Grandmothers sing, the power is building and more and more voices join, drawing in all around this special land until, in unison, everyone is singing with them.

One Grandmother steps out of the row, her face smiling now as she walks forward. She holds up her hand and speaks to all in a voice as strong as the hills around her:

The Healed Feminine comes home to light.

You can hear from the top of a hill the solitary singing of a young woman. Her crystal voice is ringing out over the land. Her hair is the colour of golden corn and she is radiant, a spring maiden. She is the divine feminine uncaught and free to roam. She has travelled through the forests and fields of Ireland. She has sat by lakes, dabbled her feet in them and spoken to the deer when they come to drink. Each strand of golden hair is the thread of a journey she has made. She is the young woman called Niamh whom we met at Knocknarea Mountain all those years ago and who was birthed out of the stars at the time of the new millennium. She is Macha's daughter. Her song resonates outwards with tremendous power.

There'll come a time on this land
When women and men will be revering.
We'll bring the ancient sacred powers
To healing and to love.[1]

You see everyone turn to look and listen to the voice of the woman singing. From the empty void, and crossing centuries of time, she is bringing the power of the ancient green land of mystical silence out into the world of today.

At a higher pitch and louder, a chorus of voices join with her, singing with the strength of the new myth being born. The song is very powerful and people are singing as loud as their voices will allow. The mountains are vibrating with the power of healed feminine light.

As the song fades into silence, all eyes turn again to the side of the hill. A second Grandmother has stepped forth and speaks:

Forgiveness takes root in the depth of the heart.

In response to this, the young woman's song rises again. Underlining, strengthening and amplifying each word the Grandmother has spoken. She is sending her song out across the land.

You can see everything around come to life. There are smiles on the faces of all of the Grandmothers. And the old women of the forests are radiant with beauty in this moment of truth that has set them free.

Tingling with the after-sound of this powerful song, you know that the land herself is singing. Feathery grasses and reeds are moving in the soft wind that blows. The trees join in the song as their top branches begin to sway. People start to move and relax. The horses that were so still in the listening are whinnying and restless. Twitching and swishing their tails and with their ears perked up, they begin to move their feet, ready to take off across the field as they hear the nuances of changing sounds. Wind shimmers across the lake and two swans fly up into the air. A whoop-whoop-whoop of their wings as they fly low across the water. It is a soft healing wave that is touching all, and all around responds. A wave, in harmony with a long-awaited birth.

As the star woman, Niamh, finishes the second rendition of her song, a young man gallops in from the woods riding a fine white horse. He slips off it and sends the horse back over towards the trees. Dressed in a fine tunic of dark-green velvet, he runs his hand through his dark hair, thick and wavy, damp with sweat. He pushes it up on his forehead and wipes his brow. The folk beside him turn to stare, wondering who he might be.

Sensing this curiosity, he turns to them and answers the unasked question: 'She is my sister and I have not seen her for many years. I have been away a long time, learning the arts of magic and medicine. With all my heart I have longed for this day when people and the whole of the land would gather to hear my sister sing like this.

'I am Fiachra, the raven boy. Together, she and I are Macha's twins. My mother would say to us when we were young: "Into the muck of Samhain's earth I gave birth to you, my precious babies." She'll be pleased to see this day at last and at Samhain time, too. And to know that when this day would come, her story comes full circle. Moreover, she does not know that I am here as it's many a year since I have met her.'

As he turns away you can see the stream of soft tears glistening on his cheeks. The man beside him wants to know more: 'But I thought the whole story was about lifting the curse from the men of Ulster?'

Fiachra turns back again and looks kindly at him.

'Yes it is, of course. But at its core is the story of healing the feminine.' He gestures up to the hill. 'It is her story, not mine. The men did not do the work to lift the curse. It was the healed light of women that did that. The soul of the men of Ulster is awakened and restored and many men are ready to receive women again in the place of their fullness.'

Macha's son pushes his way through the crowd. Raised in their midst, his easy confidence and authority is of the Dé Danann people. He himself is a skilled healer having trained with Cernunnos and the druidic teachers for many years. It is Cernunnos, the Snake God, who knows the energy lines in the land and uses them for healing.

Fiachra, reuniting with his sister and his mother on their female territory, climbs the hill and takes Niamh's hand.

She is overjoyed to see him and a rich smile lights her face. They will sing the final verse of the song together.

You can see Macha at the other side of the hill close to the horses. Her dark hair, loose around her shoulders, is streaked with silver. She looks beautiful today in a gown of emerald green, flecked with pink and gold. Perhaps her glow is a result of the release that comes when a story is finished. Seeing her son climb the hill, she gasps with surprise. He has been gone from her for many years and when she sees him take his sister's hand she raises her arms and shouts out for all to hear:

'My babies, my twins, they are here today together. Listen to their song. This is a day to give great thanks.'

And, as the woman with hair like golden corn, joins hands with her handsome brother, they finish a final round of her song together.

A chorus from all reverberates across the mountains. There is beautiful singing from the crowds who have gathered beside the sacred lake and forest at the bottom of the hill. A loud wave of cheering and clapping finishes this final piece and all present know it will restore harmony to the whole land – from east to west, from north to south.

The Healed Feminine comes home to light.
Forgiveness takes root in the depth of the heart.
The curse of ages dissolves in the waters of rebirth
That wash clean the memories in the soul of the land.
The twin blessings of joy and beauty
Ring forth their song
From the hill at Emain Macha,
And a new myth for Ireland
Is birthed across the land.

EPILOGUE
Living the Myth

One by one, throughout the year,
Events happen.
Synchronistic in their timing
They draw the threads of the story to a close.
They are like boats sailing into a harbour.
Boats that left a long time ago
On a voyage out to sea,
To a future unknown.
Through the lens of each returning vessel,
You can put your finger on where it all started.

January-December 2015

An old Donegal waltz, *The Road to Glenlough*,
Resounds clearly through the pub on New Year's Eve.
As I play it, I am taken back
To a session in Killybegs where
I first heard this tune played by a Donegal fiddler.
It was New Year's Eve in 1996.
I look round me here tonight,
In the Sean Tí in Greencastle.
A relatively small gathering for this festive eve.
As all listen attentively,
A peace descends on the room,
Bestowing warmth and belonging.
Images from eighteen years in Donegal
Appear fleetingly in front of me as I play.
Each memory dances and then dissolves.
Years and years of profound healing work
Coming gently to a close.
Return, Daughter, return.

Four of us set out on a damp summer's morning
Walking the coastal cliffs north of Glencolmcille.
Descending into the valley of Glenlough,
A deep silence pervades.
The guardian spirits watch,
As we make our way across the river and up to the old ruins.
On and on, we move across heather tufts and bracken.
At the top of the stony path that leads us out,
I stop for a final look at this holy place.
The twist in the story of the waltz named after this valley:
There is no road to Glenlough.

Honouring the memory of my young fertile years,
I throw red roses into the sea
At the Wild Mother's beach on Inis Mór.
The waves take the flowers and
Within minutes they have disappeared.
As I sing the Wild Mother's song, a heavy shower comes.
Raindrops bouncing off gentle waves.
Gratitude and release,
Shifts to joy.
Wild Mother, carry me, a wise woman I am now,
Wild Mother, carry me down to the sea.

Macha asked, all those years ago on Inis Mór,
That someday there would come a time of forgiveness.
'Put a rose at Emain Macha,' she said, 'to honour all of it.'
One pink rose onto the hill at Emain Macha
Is forgiveness for centuries of male and Church misogyny.
After placing the soft flower, I offer a prayer:
'May the new myth spread outwards from this sacred hill.
Healing wounds.
Restoring light.
Opening hearts.'

A blustery, raw morning at Cooley.
Riding with Holly and Gillian.
Thunder in the distance.
It starts to bucket with rain.
Water running down our faces,
Pouring off the horses' backs.
A river of mud is streaming down the lane.
Canter up the lane.
Hold tight against this elemental force,

It is Macha's answer to all of it.
The story is now complete.
The wild spirit of the Horse Goddess restored.

Standing at the shore of Lough Neagh,
In glorious, autumn sunshine.
The power of the Celtic Mother Goddesses,
Serene and golden, floats across the lake to me:
'Blessings given to you and your colleague Grace.'
A course at Queen's University,
Starting tomorrow morning:
The Quest for the Sacred Feminine.
Swans glide over to snap up scraps I have thrown.
They sail on by.
Grandmother Katie's spirit touches me on a breath of
wind.
She is happy that I am going to Belfast to teach.

Grandmother Katie's great-granddaughter Katy
Is married in the City Hall in Dublin.
The two mothers light candles
For the bride and groom.
Angels sing, and,
In the soft light that comes in
Through a large window in the east,
My brother John's spirit is tangibly present.
This gentle autumn light
Spreads throughout the room,
Touching all present.
Tears of joy.
A day to celebrate life.

Holly and I gallop up the lane today.
So fast, I have to stand up in the stirrups.
So perfect is the pitch,
That it seems we are moving in slow motion.
A morning of mastery.
Everything is complete.

I spend a weekend in Ballycastle with my sister Colette.
Held in the womb of memories of this precious town,
I visit again with the spirit of my mother,
Whose father died here a month before I was born.

On the morning of the winter solstice
I go for a walk on the beach.
The sand has been scoured clean
By the night-time tides rising to meet the waxing moon.
I continue to the far end and stand beside the Pans Rocks.
From across the waves,
The spirit of my mother's mother, Margaret, comes to me.
Her face radiant as she reaches out
And gives me back my infant soul.
That baby girl who nearly died at birth,
She lost a part of herself.

As I begin to walk back along the water's edge,
Crunching along the stones,
With the spray off the waves coming at me,
A small animal runs along in front, stops and glances.
Moving too quickly to get a proper look
As it disappears into the swirling tide beside a rock,
I think, a sea otter.

Sitting in the coffee shop after,
A soft winter sun comes in from the south.
Skies clear across to Fair Head.
Blue, blue, deep turquoise blue, sea,
Cold as ice, you know.
With this deepest wound healed,
The ancestral grandmothers of this land say to me:
'Begin again to live and love.'

A seagull spirals
Within the arc of a rainbow.
The sun's light catches it as it turns,
And we see the bird's flight,
White against the inky sky.
The mythic reveals itself
When you wait and watch.

Acknowledgements

I am indebted to a number of people who helped with this work – both in direct assistance with the crafting, editing and publishing process, or in their support as I was writing. I would particularly like to thank Kevin Brady, Wendy Kochman, Grace Clunie and Rose Mitchell for their invaluable input to the manuscript. They engaged with me for many hours of thoughtful and enjoyable discussion about the flow, content and detail of the writing. Their keen listening and skilled assistance helped the voice within this story to come forth clearly. They added crucial input to the editing process and, throughout the time, advised on strategies for crafting, editing and publishing. They have championed this book all the way down the track to the winning line.

Thanks are also due to Gillian Doherty Rutherford, Celia Kee Glenane, Liam Glenane, Tom Creavan, Peter Gallinagh, Carlotta Tyler, Suzanne Stevens and Jo Andersen among other friends and colleagues who have provided inspiration, listened to chapters, taken journeys to the spirit world on my behalf and offered support in many different ways. They have lifted my spirits in their commitment to seeing the work come into print.

I give my sincere thanks to the team at Guildhall Press for taking the manuscript through the final stages before printing. In particular, to Paul Hippsley for his professional advice and his highly skilled and sensitive editing. Thanks to Joe McAllister for his enthusiasm and versatile creativity in doing the cover design and overall layout. Thanks to Peter McCartney for a comprehensive proof-read and to Raymond Craig whose good humour made me smile every time I visited the office. It was a privilege to work with this team. Any remaining errors are entirely my own.

Thanks to Damien Houlahan, Ciarán McMahon, Sharon White, Rosaleen Litter, Ghilian Campbell and John Paul Coyle, staff at the Navan Centre & Fort in Armagh, who have embraced this project from the beginning and brought joy to my heart every time I went to Emain Macha for a visit.

A special thanks to Ann Khoaz who generously gave me the use of her home for extended periods of time. The peace of this sanctuary space enabled me to write with ease.

Thanks to Celia Kee Glenane for her two inspirational pieces of artwork, *Spirit Mare* and *Soul Journey*, which beautifully represent the vision of the book. Thanks to Mickey MacConnell, songwriter and Ulsterman, for permission to use the lyrics of his song *Only Our Rivers Run Free*. Thanks to poets Iggy McGovern and Tess Maginess for giving helpful advice at just the right time. I also want to express my appreciation to my fellow musicians of the Sean Tí pub in Greencastle: Paul Sloan, Mick O'Donohue, John Collins and Paddy McLaughlin, amongst others, for their friendship, humour and the many great music sessions that inspired poems and prose.

Thanks are due to John A McLaughlin for his insights into the life of tenant farmers in Inishowen in the early 1900s and thanks to Sean Beattie for his knowledge about land purchase in Inishowen. Thanks to Sony/ATV Tunes Music Publishing for permission to include lyric extracts from *Hey Jude*. Thanks also to Tro Essex Music Ltd for permission to include lyric extracts from *Those Were The Days*.

I would like to acknowledge my teachers and mentors over the past thirty years – those who have helped to hone my skills for the work described in this book. I would also like to thank my helpers, guides, teachers and Grandmothers in the spirit world. Maintaining a flow of power, love and guidance, they supported me to stay with this to the very end. Sincere thanks also to the people who attended talks, workshops, retreats, pilgrimages and meditations over the years, as without them, there would be no story to write.

A word of thanks to the scholars of Celtic mythology and literature who have translated and interpreted the old stories making them available for contemporary use.

To my family and the wider circle of my friends, heartfelt thanks for your love and support. Light and love to you always.

Notes and References

Preface

1. JA MacCulloch, *Celtic Mythology*, (2nd edition), London: Constable, 1992.

2. The name of the city of Armagh, in the south of Ulster, comes from the Irish: *Ard Mhacha*, which means the 'high place of Macha'. The name of Armagh was associated with Macha before St Patrick and before it became the Christian ecclesiastical capital of Ireland.

3. Navan Fort is a large circular earthworks two miles west of Armagh city. There is an interpretive and education centre close by, with meeting spaces and dedicated areas for audio-visual presentations on the history of Ulster and the myths of the Ulster Cycle. (See Navan Centre & Fort: www.navan.com)

4. Marion Woodman, a Jungian analyst trained at the CG Jung Institute in Switzerland, was a pioneer of the search for the conscious feminine from the 1980s to date. Her numerous books provide great insights into the pathways and myths that can help women to access their authentic selves through dream analysis and body work. She did ground-breaking work to connect the human body with soul and spirit.

5. The traditional associations of the five provinces of Ireland were: Ulster with war, Leinster with prosperity, Connaught with wisdom and Munster with music. Mide – the fifth province, with the Hill of Uisneach in the centre – was associated with the magical Otherworld.

6. C Gallardo, *The Mechanics of the Transcendent Function*, extended essay on E Psychotherapist, 2004, (online) available from: www.epsychotherapist.org/ therapist/mydocuments/Transcendent%20Function%202005.doc (Accessed: 16 March 2017).

7. The *Belfast Telegraph* (newspaper), 4 March 2017, (online) available from: www.belfasttelegraph.co.uk/news/northern-ireland-assembly-election (Accessed: 6 March 2017).

BOOK ONE
One: Calling Macha Home

1. *Emhain Mhacha* is the correct Irish spelling for the 'Twins of Macha'. When translated phonetically into English this became 'Navan' Fort giving the name to the ancient royal site in County Armagh. I refer to Emain Macha throughout the book as this spelling is more commonly used.

2. The Ulster Myths – in T Kinsella, (trans.) *The Táin*, from the Irish epic story *Táin Bó Cuailgne*, Dublin: Dolmen, 1968.

3. P McCana, *Celtic Mythology*, London: Chancellor Press, 1997, pp.86-88.

4. Twins of Macha, as above, note 1.

5. JA MacCulloch, *op. cit.*, pp.42-49.

6. Story adapted from: M Heaney, *Over Nine Waves: A Book of Irish Legends*, London: Faber and Faber, 1994.

7. M Condren, *The Serpent and the Goddess: Women, Religion and Power in Celtic Ireland*, San Francisco: Harper & Row, 1989, p.32.

8. M Heaney, *op. cit.*, p.68.

Two: Conversations at Emain Macha

1. RJ Stewart, *Celtic Gods and Goddesses*, (5th edition), London: Blandford, 1994, p.54. (Epona was the Horse Goddess of Celtic Europe. Macha was the Horse Goddess of the Tuatha Dé Danann in Ireland.)

2. Churching of Women. There are contrasting opinions on whether this was a ritual of blessing or the cleansing of women who were in some way tarnished after giving birth. It ceased to be carried out in the Catholic Church in the 1940s. The previous rites for 'churching' the mother forty days after childbirth are now incorporated into the sacrament of baptism. C Murray, New Advent, 2012, (online) available from: http://www.newadvent.org/cathen/03761a. htm (Accessed: 28 October 2013) and N Knödel, University of Durham, 1995, (online) available from: http://users.ox.ac.uk/%7Emikef/church.html#intro (Accessed: 28 October 2013).

3. The Rose Quartz Day – 7 July 2007 in Derry, N Ireland – was the first *Light in Ireland* event. It was organised by the Vibrational Healing Foundation, London, UK, in conjunction with Maureen Hetherington and a number of qualified Energy Practitioners dedicated to peace in the North of Ireland.

Three: A Deeper Story

1. Ulster had nine counties before partition in 1921. The counties Monaghan, Donegal and Cavan became part of the Free State and the other six counties became the province of Northern Ireland and remained within the UK. See J Bardon, *A History of Ulster*, (updated edition), Belfast: Blackstaff Press, 2000, pp.478-9.

2. T'ai Chi is an ancient practice of movement meditation that originated in China. The exercises that I use are from Qi Gong, a variation of T'ai Chi.

Four: Fertile Blood

1. Kedzie Penfield is a dance and movement therapist based in Edinburgh, Scotland.

Five: Meeting Macha

1. K Carter (Fitzpatrick), *Mother Goddess*, *Aisling* Quarterly Magazine, Bealtaine, Issue No. 6, 1992.

2. Paul Rebillot (1931-2010) pioneered a school of ground-breaking work by combining the skills of drama, myth, gestalt therapy and ritual to create archetypal journeys for personal transformation through ritual enactment. The *Lover's Journey* was one of his archetypal structures.

3. *A Woman's Heart*, (Audio CD), various female artists, August 1992.

4. Paul Rebillot set up the North American School of Gestalt and Experiential Training (NASGET) in 1992 to train facilitators in gestalt practice and the art of structure in the areas of myth, gestalt, drama and ritual.

5. Carol Proudfoot-Edgar, California, USA, was a faculty member of NASGET and taught ceremony, shamanic drumming and journeying, communication with the spirits of nature and ways of walking between the unseen worlds.

6. The *An Charraig* lifestyle: Living a simple, self-sufficient, spiritual lifestyle involving a vision of developing right relationships with nature and with others and rooted in the Irish cultural and spiritual tradition. (Tess O'Maoildhia, pers. comm., February 2017.)

Six: Beyond the Waves

1. RTÉ: Radio Telefis Éireann – Ireland's National Television and Radio Broadcaster.

2. C Pinkola Estés, *Women Who Run With the Wolves: Myths and Stories of the Wild Woman Archetype*, New York: Ballantine, 1992.

3. *The River is Flowing* – traditional chant for the Mother Goddess. Used in the 1990s by many women's groups on a quest for the divine feminine.

4. *Samhain* is the Celtic Fire Festival of New Year and takes place on 1 November. As in all of these Fire Festivals, it is celebrated on the evening before. It is the Hallowe'en celebration in modern time.

Seven: Transformation

1. *Imbolc* is the Celtic Fire Festival of spring, which is celebrated on 1 February. It is associated with the Goddess Brigid and called St Brigid's Day. On the eve of Imbolc, rushes are still collected in many parts of Ireland to make the 'Brigid' crosses.

2. A series of three articles on Celtic myth, Jungian psychology and healing, *Aisling* Quarterly Magazine, Imbolc, Bealtaine & Lúghnasa, Issue Nos. 9, 10 & 11, 1992.

3. B Mauger, *The Inner Marriage: Love, Heartbreak and the Search for Wholeness*, IAHIP, *Inside Out*, Issue No. 56, Winter 2008, (online) available from: http:// iahip.org/inside-out/issue-56-winter-2008/the-inner-marriage-love-heartbreak-and-the-search-for-wholeness (Accessed: 23 February 2017).

Eight: Emerging New

1. *Bealtaine* is the Celtic Fire Festival of the summer time. Celebrated on 1 May, it was traditionally associated with fertility, marriages and abundance.

2. *Ancient Mother*, a traditional Goddess chant. See *Ancient Mother* (album) by Robert Gass & On Wings of Song, USA, 1993.

3. *Return Again*, traditional chant. See *Songs of Healing* (album) by Robert Gass & On Wings of Song, USA, 1992.

4. *We are the Walking Breath*, a chant from Kathie Prince, Voice Teacher, 1991.

5. *The Celtic Goddess Mandala* is a mythic structure and journey designed and used by K Fitzpatrick for over twenty years to teach women who are searching for the wholeness of their inner feminine.

6. Carol Proudfoot-Edgar, California, USA, pioneered Bear Medicine as a shamanic practice for women (1990–). Her intention for this work was to reclaim the wisdom and ways of the female shamans of former times. Bear Medicine is an embodied path and some of the practices are for strengthening the female body, recovering instincts and finding alignment with the ancestors. With adequate grounding in the body, along with a connection to spirit helpers, women can do very effective spiritual healing and energy work with individuals, groups and with the land.

7. *Tonnta, the Music of the Waves*, 1995. A cassette recording produced by the people of the island to keep a historical record of the musicians and singers of Inis Mór, County Galway.

Ten: Immram

1. *Celtic Connections: Journeys for Women* by Carlotta Tyler and Suzanne Stevens (1998-2002). These journeys in Ireland were reinstated in May 2015 and take place in Killarney, County Kerry, every two years.

2. M Heaney, *op. cit.*, p.126.

3. *Hey Jude* words and music by John Lennon and Paul McCartney © 1968. Reproduced by permission of Sony/ATV Tunes Music Publishing, London WIF 9LD.

Twelve: Bear Medicine

1. Extract from the song: *Only Our Rivers Run Free*, M MacConnell ©1965. Printed with permission from the author.

2. Ibid.

3. R Kee, *Ireland: A History*, London: Weidenfeld and Nicolson, 1980, pp.137-8.

Fourteen: Macha's Joy

1. Manannán mac Lir was the God of the sea in Celtic mythology. The white horses of the waves were said to be Manannán's steeds. (P McCana, *op. cit.*, p.69.)

Epilogue: A New Millennium

1. *Brigid: Soulsmith for a New Millennium*. Weekend celebration for Imbolc, the Institute of Feminism and Religion, Stranmillis College, Belfast, 2000.
2. The *Soulsmith Song*, from a shamanic journey to the spirit of Brigid for the Imbolc celebration in Belfast.

BOOK TWO
Two: A Shadow Passes Over

1. N Pennick, *Celtic Sacred Landscapes*, London: Thames and Hudson, 1996, p.13. An excellent book about the indwelling soul in the land, stones, trees, wells and mountains. In the practice and training of shamanism, 'soul loss' refers to the loss of the vital energy or life force within individuals, all living creatures, plants and the land itself. Soul retrieval is the healing technique used to call the soul back home.

2. M Dames, *Mythic Ireland*, London: Thames and Hudson, 1992, pp.247-258.

3. JA McLaughlin, *Carrowmenagh: History of a Donegal Village*, Inishowen: 2001. (pers. comm., September 2013.)

4. JA McLaughlin, *A History of Falmore House, Gleneely*, (booklet), Carndonagh, Foyle Press, 2009.

5. There were several Land Purchase Acts put into place by the British Government in the late 1880s and the early1900s. The process for tenant farmers to buy out their holdings extended over a period of fifty years. This was dependent on their ability to secure money or a mortgage for the purchase. By 1924, most families in north Inishowen had become the legal owners of their holdings. (Sean Beattie, pers. comm., March 2017.)

6. N Pennick, *op. cit.*, pp.48 & 77.

7. J Bardon, *op. cit.*, pp.476-9.

Three: Memories

1. P Lawlor, *The Burnings 1920*, Cork: Mercier, 2009, pp.115-152.

2. Extract from the song: *Come Back, Paddy Reilly, To Ballyjamesduff* by Percy French, 1912.

Four: Rose Quartz

1. First International Shamanic Gathering organised by Tending Sacred Circles, at Oracle, Arizona, April 2000.

2. The Vibrational Healing Foundation, London, UK, founded by Henriette Maasdijk, has been providing expert tuition and training in subtle energy medicine, the healing arts and inner development since 1996.

Five: Child of Lisburn

1. B Mackey, *Lisburn, The Town and its People 1873-1973*, Belfast: Blackstaff Press, 2000, p.14.

Six: Healing Peace

1. *International Peace Gathering*, Hope Springs Institute, Peebles, Ohio, USA, June 2010.

2. P Lawlor's book *The Burnings 1920 (op. cit.)* was launched by author Glenn Patterson at Lisburn City Library on Thursday 12 March 2009.

3. K Haddick-Flynn, *Orangeism: The Making of a Tradition*, Dublin: Wolfhound, 1999, p.331 and J Bardon, *op. cit.*, pp.504-5.

Seven: Music With the Men of Ulster

1. Extract from the song: *Those Were The Days*, G Raskin © 1968. Reproduced with permission of Tro Essex Music Ltd, London SW10 0SZ.

2. *Lúghnasa* is the Celtic Fire Festival of the harvest and is celebrated in modern times on 1 August and as 'Lammas' festivals throughout the month of August. It is named after *Lugh*, the God of the harvest of the Tuatha Dé Danann. See B Day, *Chronicle of Celtic Folk Customs*, London: Hamlyn, 2000, pp.128-148.

3. K Fitzpatrick, *Fruits of the Harvest*, Celtic Meditation, 2012.

Eight: Autumn Peace

1. K Kennicott Davis, *The Little Drummer Boy*, 1941. (A popular Christmas carol.)

Nine: Light of Brigid

1. *The Soulsmith Song, op. cit..*

2. K Carter (Fitzpatrick), *Healing the Split*, *Aisling* Quarterly Magazine, Lúghnasa, Issue No. 11, 1993.

Ten: Angels in Belfast

1. Association for Coaching (AC) 2nd Ireland National Conference, *Back to the Future* hosted at the Belfast Met, Titanic Quarter, Belfast, N Ireland, 26 April 2013.

2. Dr Carole Pemberton, executive coach, resilience expert and author, is based in the UK. She is a visiting professor at the University of Ulster Business School.

3. Brian Smyth is the managing director of *Maybe International* a creative consultancy dedicated to 'realise possibilities' and help organisations to 'manage to be human'.

4. Leonard Bernstein (1918-1990) was an American composer, conductor, author, music lecturer, and pianist. He was among the first conductors born and educated in the US to receive worldwide acclaim. His fame derived from his long tenure as the music director of the of the New York Philharmonic, from his conducting of concerts with most of the world's leading orchestras, and from his music for *West Side Story*. https://en.wikipedia.org/wiki/Leonard_Bernstein (Accessed: February 2017).

5. S Earle, *The Galway Girl*, (song) recorded with Sharon Shannon, musician, for the album *Transcendental Blues*, 2000.

6. Extract from the song: *Are Ye Right There, Michael?*, Percy French, 1897.

Eleven: Forgiveness

1. *Martin McCrossan Tours*, Derry, N Ireland.

2. T Kelly, W Kelly and K Hasson, (The Bogside Artists, Derry) *Death of Innocence*, 1999, one of twelve wall murals, known as The People's Gallery.

3. INCORE International Conflict Research Institute at the University of Ulster, Magee Campus, Northland Road, Londonderry BT48 7JA.

4. K Fitzpatrick, *Spirit of the Wind*, Celtic Meditation, 2013.

Thirteen: Soul of the Horse

1. K Fitzpatrick, *Spirit of Water*, Celtic Meditation, 2013.

2. Cooley Equestrian Centre, Cooley, Moville, Inishowen, County Donegal. AIRE approved centre and also incorporates RDAI (therapeutic riding for the disabled) into its programme. Run by G Doherty Rutherford and her family.

Fifteen: Winter

1. G Doherty Rutherford (pers. comm., September 2013).

Sixteen: Grandmothers of the Mountains

1. The images for this vision of sequence riding were taken from the experience of sequence riding at Cooley Equestrian Centre created and directed by G Doherty Rutherford.

2. There was an ancient sacred site at Cooley Cross and later it became a monastic site with St Finian of Moville as its leader. Believed to be connected energetically to the other sacred stone sites in Inishowen. Article by S Beattie, (online) available from: http://movilleinishowen.com/history-genealogy/cooley-graveyard/ and details at http://curiousireland.ie/cooley-cross/ (Accessed: February 2017).

Seventeen: The Silence Before Birth

1. This song was given to me by the 'star spirits' during a Vision Quest that I did at Murlough Bay, north Antrim, in June 1999. T Johnson from Pennsylvania, who has been leading Vision Quests since 1995, facilitated the ten-day event.

IRELAND

Cruit
Island

Moville

Lough
Foyle

Ballycastle

Derry City

ULSTER

Killybegs

Belfast

Sligo

Emain
Macha

CONNAUGHT

Hill of
Uisneach

Galway
City

Dublin

Inis Mór

LEINSTER

MUNSTER

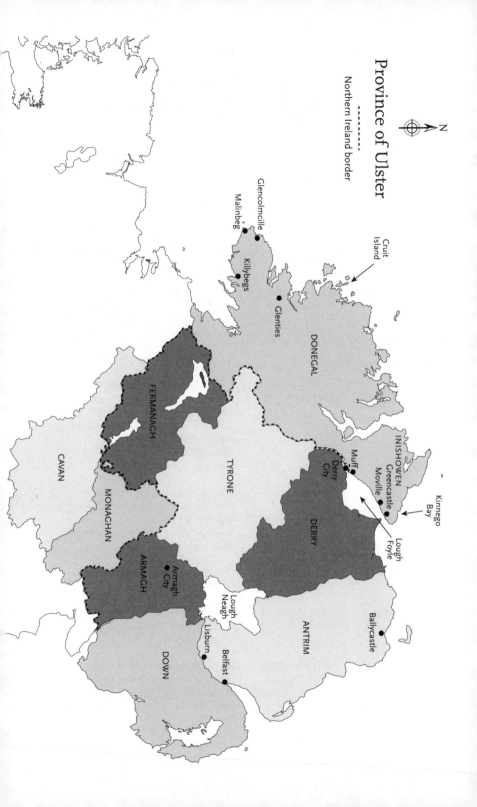

Province of Ulster

.... Northern Ireland border

N

Cruit
Island

Glencolmcille
Malinbeg

Killybegs

Glenties

DONEGAL

INISHOWEN

FERMANAGH

TYRONE

Muff

Derry
City

Greencastle
Moville

Kinnego
Bay

CAVAN

MONAGHAN

DERRY

Lough
Foyle

Ballycastle

ARMAGH

Armagh
City

Lough
Neagh

ANTRIM

DOWN

Lisburn

Belfast

Story Timeline

Time period	Home base for the author	Workshops & events significant to the story
1990	Strandhill, County Sligo	Environmental Arts Project using mountain landscapes, based in Calry, County Sligo, Aug '90-Aug '91.
1991-1992	Ballygrania, Collooney, County Sligo	*Great Mother* workshop in St Angela's, April '91. Writing the *Mother Goddess* article for the *Aisling* Magazine, April '91. Jungian psychology course in Dublin, Sept '91-June '92.
1992-1993	Inis Mór, Aran Islands, County Galway	Travel to California for a preparatory workshop for the Rebillot training in the art of creating gestalt and mythic structures, Aug '92. Writing articles on Jungian psychology & Celtic myth for the *Aisling* Magazine, Jan '93.
1993-1994	Inis Mór	Four-year training with the North American School of Gestalt and Experiential Teaching, with Paul Rebillot, begins in the US, Aug '93. *Celtic Goddesses Mandala* workshop, May '94.
1994-1995	Inis Mór	Three-year training in Bear Medicine & Shamanism, with Carol Proudfoot-Edgar, begins in the US, Sept '94. Music recording of the island heritage, April '95.
1995-96	Galway City & Inis Mór	Finishing on the island. Playing music during summer of '95.
1996-97	Killybegs, County Donegal	Brigid's Day workshop: *Birthing That Which is New Within*, Glencolmcille, County Donegal, Feb '97.
1997-98	Muff, Inishowen, County Donegal	Derry City, working with various organisations committed to the healing of trauma within the North of Ireland. 1st Glenties workshop and pilgrimage, Sept '98.

Time period	Home base for the author	Workshops & events significant to the story
1998-99	Kinnego Bay, Inishowen, County Donegal	2nd Glenties workshop, 2nd pilgrimage, Bear Medicine retreat and *Samhain Bear* workshop, Sept-Nov '99.
1999-2000	Kinnego Bay	Brigid in Belfast – *Soulsmith for the New Millennium*, Jan 2000. Shamanic Gathering in Arizona, World Map for healing, April 2000.
2001	Kinnego Bay	Bear Medicine healing ceremony at Cruit Island, County Donegal, April 2001.
2004-07		A gap period. Author took a sabbatical away from Donegal.
2008-09	Moville, County Donegal	Negotiating a site and drawing up plans to build a house at Tirrion (near to Kinnego Bay, five miles from Moville)
2010	Moville & Tirrion	Lease the little house at Tirrion and do renovations, March-July 2010. Keynote speaker at the International Peace Gathering at Hope Springs, Ohio, US, June 2010.
2011	Moville & Tirrion	Celtic Meditations begin at the little house, July 2011.
2012	Moville & Tirrion	*Calling Macha Home* – presentation at Navan Centre & Fort, County Armagh, Feb '12.
2013	Moville & Tirrion	*Light of Brigid* – presentation at Navan Centre & Fort, County Armagh, Feb '13. Association for Coaching (AC) Conference in Belfast, April '13. Celtic Meditations – *Spirit of the Wind*, May '13 and *Spirit of Water*, July '13. Begin horse riding at Cooley Stables, Moville, July '13.
2014	Moville & Sligo	Crafting the book on Macha and finishing the mythic story.
2015	Moville & Sligo	Completing the book, writing the epilogue.

Glossary of Mythic Names

Brigid
A Mother Goddess of fire, spring and new birth. Traditionally a triple Goddess, Brigid was associated with smithcraft, poetry and healing.

Cernunnos
A God of the Tuatha Dé Danann who is associated with the snake. He is guardian of the energy patterns and life force of the land and will assist with the energetic cleansing of the soul of the land.

Cruinniuc
The human man whom Macha chooses as a husband and takes up residence with him in his prosperous farm in Ulster. He is the father of her twins.

Cú Chulainn
Champion warrior of Ulster. As a son of Lugh, and therefore partly a divine being, he is the only man not affected by Macha's curse. His mother was Dectera, a sister of King Conchobhar.

Danu
The Mother Goddess of the tribes of Danu – The Tuatha Dé Danann.

Fiachra
In this story he is the son of Macha. In the legends of the Tuatha Dé Danann he was one of the four children of Lir transformed into swans for 900 years. His name means raven.

Immram
An Immram is a heroic journey or spiritual passage out to sea and to mystical islands beyond the ninth wave. The plural is Immrama.

King Conchobhar mac Nessa
The King of Ulster after Macha's time. He is a key character in the myths of the Ulster Cycle. His warriors are struck down with the pangs of labour when they go into battle – the legacy of Macha's curse.

Macha
The main character in the story. A Mother Goddess and closely allied with the power of horses, she is a guide to women for wildness of spirit, fertility and the transformation of curse to blessing.

Manannán mac Lir
The God of the sea. He guards the threshold to the mystical
Otherworld that is out beyond the ninth wave.

Medhbh
Warrior Queen of Connaught. She went to war with the men of
Ulster for the brown bull of Cooley. *Táin Bó Cuailgne* is the epic
story of her battles.

Morrígan
Known in her triple form as the Morrígan, she is the Goddess of
war and the one who can assist the transformation of conflict and
bring peace and harmony. She is one of the four Celtic Goddesses,
along with Danu, Brigid and Macha, that form the circle of the
Celtic Mandala. They are all Goddesses of the Tuatha Dé Danann.

Niamh
In this story she is a daughter of Macha. Originally, Niamh of the
golden hair appears as a daughter of Manannán mac Lir. She was
Niamh of the starlit heavens and her name means radiance, lustre,
and brightness.

The Ninth Wave
A magical place out in the ocean where Manannán mac Lir guards
the threshold to the realms of the Sídhe. Many of the old legends
tell of heroic sea voyages to the mystical Otherworld beyond the
ninth wave. The voyages were undertaken to seek inspiration and
they usually incorporated visits to the mystical islands of the far
west and numerous challenges. These are known in the literature
as the Immrama tales.

The Sídhe
When the Gaels invaded Ireland and brought with them a Celtic
culture (in the late Bronze Age around 500BC), it is said that the
Tuatha Dé Danann went underground into the sacred stone sites,
rivers, wells, mountains and out beyond the ninth wave. They
became known as the Sídhe (pronounced *Shee*) or 'Fair Ones' and
reside to this day in the invisible worlds of a parallel universe.

Tuatha Dé Danann
A mystical race of divine beings that invaded Ireland and took
control from the Formorians at the second Battle of Moytura.
The name means the tribes of Danu. They are the children of the
Goddess Danu. It is said that they came from the northern islands
and, skilled in the druidic arts, brought with them the knowledge
of the stars. Also referred to as the Dé Danann and the Dananns.

The Four Seasonal Celtic Fire Festivals

These mark out the quarter days of the year. They were celebrated in Celtic culture as a way of marking the shifts in cosmic energy at each season. These are all auspicious times and many of the legends are said to take place at these special times.

Imbolc

Celebrated on 1 February as the first day of spring. Associated with the Goddess Brigid. It was a time of new birth and the emerging from winter darkness. The name means ewe's milk, a reference to the birth of the first lambs of the season.

Bealtaine

Celebrated on 1 May as the first day of summer. A mystical time when the Sídhe were abroad and their magic was felt in the air. Named after Bel, the God of fire.

Lúghnasa

Celebrated on 1 August as the first day of autumn. A time when the light began to fade and the harvests were being brought in. Named after Lugh, the God of the harvest.

Samhain

Celebrated on 1 November as an honouring of the dead and the beginning of winter's darkness. It was a magical time when the veils were thin and all manner of spirits were abroad. It marked the Celtic New Year.

Bibliography

Celtic Mythology & Spirituality

P Beresford Ellis, *The Celts, A Brief History of,* (revised edition), London: Robinson, 2003.

P Clancy, (editor), *Celtic Threads: Exploring the Wisdom of Our Heritage,* Dublin: Veritas, 1999.

G Clunie & T Maginess, *The Celtic Spirit and Literature,* Dublin: The Columba Press, 2015.

M Dames, *Mythic Ireland,* London: Thames and Hudson, 1992.

B Day, *Chronicle of Celtic Folk Customs,* London: Hamlyn, 2000.

F Delaney, *Legends of The Celts,* London: Hodder & Stoughton, 1989.

M Heaney, *Over Nine Waves: A Book of Irish Legends,* London: Faber and Faber, 1994.

E Hull, *Cuchulain The Hound of Ulster,* London: George G Harrap & Co., 1911.

T Kinsella, (trans.) *The Táin,* from the Irish epic story *Táin Bó Cuailgne,* Dublin: Dolmen, 1968.

P McCana, *Celtic Mythology,* London: Chancellor Press, 1997.

JA MacCulloch, *Celtic Mythology,* (2nd edition), London: Constable, 1992.

N Pennick, *Celtic Sacred Landscapes,* London: Thames and Hudson, 1996.

RJ Stewart, *Celtic Gods and Goddesses,* (5th edition), London: Blandford, 1994.

D Whelan, *Ever Ancient, Ever New: Celtic Spirituality in the 21st Century,* Dublin: Original Writing, 2010.

Sacred Feminine, Women and Mythology

A Bancroft, *Origins Of The Sacred: The Spiritual Journey in Western Tradition,* London: Routledge & Kegan Paul, 1987.

P Beresford Ellis, *Celtic Women: Women in Celtic Society and Literature,* London: Constable, 1995.

M Caldecott, *Women in Celtic Myth: Tales of Extraordinary Women from the Ancient Celtic Tradition,* Vermont: Destiny Books, 1992.

M Condren, *The Serpent and the Goddess: Women, Religion and Power in Celtic Ireland,* San Francisco: Harper & Row, 1989.

L Shlain, *The Alphabet Versus The Goddess: The Conflict Between Word and Image*, New York: Viking Penguin, 1998.

M Sjöö & B Mor, *The Great Cosmic Mother: Rediscovering The Religion of the Earth*, San Francisco: Harper Collins, 1991.

The Feminine in Jungian Psychology

ME Harding, *Woman's Mysteries: The inner life of women revealed in religious myth and ritual*, London: Rider, 1998.

C Pinkola Estés, *Women Who Run With the Wolves: Myths and Stories of the Wild Woman Archetype*, New York: Ballantine, 1992.

M Woodman & E Dickson, *Dancing in the Flames: The Dark Goddess in the Transformation of Conscious*, Dublin: Gill & Macmillan, 1996.

M Woodman, *Addiction to Perfection: The Still Unravished Bride*, Toronto: Inner City Books, 1982.

_____, *The Pregnant Virgin: A Process of Psychological Transformation*, Toronto: Inner City Books, 1985.

_____, *The Ravaged Bridegroom: Masculinity in Women*, Toronto: Inner City Books, 1990.

Healing Theatre & Myth

S Jennings, *Introduction to Dramatherapy, Theatre and Healing – Ariadne's Ball of Thread*, London: Jessica Kingsley, 1997.

P Rebillot, with M Kay, *The Call to Adventure: Bringing the Hero's Journey to Daily Life*, San Francisco: HarperSanFrancisco, 1993.

T Sepinuck, *Theatre of Witness*, London: Jessica Kingsley, 2013.

History of Ulster

J Bardon, *A History of Ulster*, (updated edition), Belfast: Blackstaff Press, 2000.

TP Coogan, *Ireland In the Twentieth Century*, London: Arrow Books, 2004.

K Haddick-Flynn, *Orangeism: The Making of a Tradition*, Dublin: Wolfhound, 1999.

M Jess, *The Orange Order*, Dublin: The O'Brien Press, 2007.

R Kee, *Ireland: A History*, London: Weidenfeld and Nicolson, 1980.

J Kelly, *Bonfires on the Hillside: An Eyewitness Account of Political Upheaval in Northern Ireland*, Belfast: Fountain, 1995.

P Lawlor, *The Burnings 1920*, Cork: Mercier, 2009.

B Mackey, *Lisburn, The Town and its People 1873-1973*, Belfast: Blackstaff Press, 2000.

S McKay, *Northern Protestants: An Unsettled People*, (2nd edition), Belfast: Blackstaff Press, 2005.

JA McLaughlin, *Carrowmenagh: History of a Donegal Village*, Inishowen: 2001.

Crystal Healing, Shamanism & Meditation

T Cowan, *Fire in the Head: Shamanism and the Celtic Spirit*, New York: Harper Collins, 1993.

____, *Shamanism as a Spiritual Practice for Daily Life*, New York: Crossing Press, 1996.

H Maasdijk, *Crystals & Healing for Everyone*, London: VHF, 2004.

S Roman, *Spiritual Growth: Being Your Higher Self*, California: HJ Kramer Inc., 1989.

E Tolle, *The Power Of Now: A Guide to Spiritual Enlightenment*, (2nd edition), California: New World Library, 2004.

A Villoldo, *Shaman, Healer, Sage*, London: Bantam Books, 2000.

Horses & Healing

R Isaacson, *The Horse Boy: The True Story of a Father's Miraculous Journey to Heal his Son*, London: Penguin, 2009.

____, *The Long Ride Home: The Extraordinary Journey of Healing that Changed a Child's life*, London: Penguin, 2014.

L Kohanov, *The Tao of Equus: A Woman's Journey of Healing and Transformation through the Way of the Horse*, California: New World Library, 2001.

____, *Riding Between the Worlds: Expanding our Potential Through the Way of the Horse*, California: New World Library, 2003.

Other

J Feehan et al., *The Book of Aran: The Aran Islands, County Galway*, Kinvara, Galway: Tír Eolas, 1994.

Homer, (trans.) EV Rieu, *The Odyssey*, (3rd edition), London: Penguin, 2003.

JC Zinker, *Creative Process in Gestalt Therapy*, New York: Random House, 1978.

About the Author

Kate Fitzpatrick has studied and taught the spirituality and healing power of Celtic myth for over twenty-five years. She guides retreats and sacred journeys around Ireland. She was born in Lisburn in County Antrim in 1958 and grew up in the North of Ireland. She went to Bradford University in the 1970s to study Environmental Science and afterwards moved to the west of Ireland to live in County Sligo. In the 1980s, along with several other artists, she pioneered the creation of outdoor performance and healing theatre from themes and stories within Celtic mythology. She has a certificate in Jungian psychology, is a trained Gestalt and Experiential teacher and a certified practitioner of Shamanism and Bear Medicine. Kate lives in Inishowen in County Donegal where she plays music on the fiddle in local sessions, likes hiking and horse-riding and enjoys time in the company of friends and family.